# MUSASHI'S

# BOOK
# OF
# FIVE
# RINGS

D0094009

MUSASHI'S

# BOOK
# OF
# FIVE
# RINGS

*The Definitive Interpretation*
*of Miyamoto Musashi's*
*Classic Book of Strategy*

STEPHEN F. KAUFMAN, HANSHI 10th DAN

TUTTLE PUBLISHING
Tokyo • Rutland, Vermont • Singapore

Published by Tuttle Publishing, an imprint of Periplus Editions (HK) Ltd., with editorial offices at 364 Innovation Drive, North Clarendon, Vermont 05759 U.S.A. and 61 Tai Seng Avenue, #02-12, Singapore 534167.

Library of Congress Cataloging-in-Publication Data

Kaufman, Steve, 1939–
    Musashi's book of five rings : the definitive interpretation of Miyamoto Musashi's classic book of strategy / Stephen F. Kaufman.
    Kaufman, Steve, 1939– Martial Artist's book of five rings.
    Miyamoto, Musashi, 1584–1645. Gorin no sho. English.
        p. cm.
    ISBN: 0–8048–3520–9 (pbk)
    Previous title : Martial artist's book of five rings. 1994.
    Miyamoto, Musashi, 1584–1645. Gorin no sho.
    Military art and science—Early works to 1800.
    Swordplay—Japan—Early works to 1800.
    U101 .K38    2004                                    2003054039

ISBN 978-0-8048-3520-6

Distributed by:

**North America, Latin America & Europe**
Tuttle Publishing
364 Innovation Drive
North Clarendon, VT 05759-9436 U.S.A.
Tel: 1 (802) 773-8930
Fax: 1 (802) 773-6993
info@tuttlepublishing.com
www.tuttlepublishing.com

**Asia Pacific**
Berkeley Books Pte. Ltd.
61 Tai Seng Avenue #02-12
Singapore 534167
Tel: (65) 6280-1330
Fax: (65) 6280-6290
inquiries@periplus.com.sg
www.periplus.com

**Japan**
Tuttle Publishing
Yaekari Building, 3rd Floor
5-4-12 Osaki
Shinagawa-ku
Tokyo 141-0032
Tel: (81) 03 5437-0171
Fax: (81) 03 5437-0755
tuttle-sales@gol.com

**Indonesia**
PT Java Books Indonesia
Kawasan Industri Pulogadung
Jl. Rawa Gelam IV No. 9
Jakarta 13930
Tel: (62) 21 4682-1088
Fax: (62) 20 461-0207
cs@javabooks.co.id

15 14 13 12 11 10        18 17 16 15 14
Text design by Jill Winitzer
Printed in the United States of America

TUTTLE PUBLISHING ® is a registered trademark of Tuttle Publishing, a division of Periplus Editions (HK) Ltd.

*This book is dedicated to my father*
*Jack Kaufman*
*a  warrior in his own right*
*and to the legacy of*
*Miyamoto Musashi*

# CONTENTS

# PREFACE

M usashi is well known to most martialists. He is considered the *Kensei*, sword-saint of Japan. While his teachings are essentially centered around swordsmanship, his teachings fall without question into the domain of study for practitioners of all the martial arts, including karate, judo, Western fencing and other killing forms as well, but, only if they are used to take life in combat.

*The Book of Five Rings* is Miyamoto Musashi's teaching on the art of strategy in combat based on swordsmanship. It must be understood that whether or not you practice the martial arts or use the teachings for other disciplines, there are profound truths to be gleaned from this work, Musashi's legacy.

My own personal involvement in the art of karate for nearly forty years, along with my ten-year study of the "Rings," has led me to take the responsibility of interpreting these teachings for the martialist who wishes to understand the true "Way."

This is a profound work on life and death in combat. It is not for the immature. I do not advocate the taking of life for any reason. Keep in mind that Musashi's work was done at a time when mortal combat was a way of life. The teachings of Musashi, and this interpretation are to explain the principles and philosophy of a warrior's life in ancient Japan.

# ABOUT THE TRANSLATION

This is not another book about Japanese business strategy. There is a significant difference between not getting a deal signed and having your head cut off. Business is mental. War is mental *and* physical. The true warrior has no difficulty understanding this difference regardless of all the hype suggesting that "business is war." It absolutely is *not*.

This is a book for "martialists." Not martial artists. The concept of "art" can lead to a misunderstanding of the warrior's purpose and preclude a subjective relationship to form and function. For, paradoxically, the warrior is all passion although he shows none and "kills" without hesitation. The reality is one of neither subjectivity nor objectivity.

Development of technique is essential to understanding of purpose. Once a specific technique has been understood, the warrior stops using it on a conscious level because in combat having a conscious identity imposes limitations. Knowing how to do something and actually doing it are not at all the same thing. Taking a life is not the same as taking money. This fundamental premise is the reason why samurai despised the merchant class even while understanding the need for the merchant mentality. Cold-blooded businessmen, however, do not understand the true Way of the warrior.

The majority of translations of Musashi's work available on the market are little more than intellectual exercises in translating Japanese to English. They do not adequately express the feeling required to study life and death confrontations and therefore fall short of the mark. The present work has been done with the purpose of clearing up the misconceptions of naive Westerners and Easterners as to the "real" purpose of the Five Rings. It explains in depth, with additional definition, the truths that must be comprehended before it is possible to come to terms with the teachings of Musashi. It is therefore to be studied as a "universal" explanation.

With deep reverence and profound homage to the master, I take full responsibility for the interpretation of all concepts presented herein.

Steve Kaufman, Hanshi, 10th Dan

# MUSASHI'S

# BOOK OF FIVE RINGS

# INTRODUCTION

My name is Miyamoto Musashi. I have killed over sixty men in fights and duels. When I was sixty years of age I looked back upon my life and in a flash of wisdom, realized that all my victories were based on either great luck, an innate ability, or perhaps the fact that the methods of other schools were inadequate.

When I came to terms with my own skills and abilities, the realities of what I had accomplished held me to a higher principle that left me no choice but to depart from the commerce of the world, seek isolation, and tear my soul apart so that I could examine what I already seemed to know instinctively. I practiced and meditated constantly until I came to understand the workings of the spirit.

I am considered to be the greatest swordsman Japan has ever had. It was during my fights and duels that I developed my own style of two-sword fighting. Although I was committed to my sword, I was also dedicated to learning painting, sculpture, and poetry. I instinctively felt it necessary to understand the arts and be accomplished in them. But my prime focus was on swordsmanship. I was not a particularly religious person, although I know of Buddhism, Shintoism, and Confucianism and am aware of their tenets.

What will be changed in my teachings with the passing of time cannot be known. There are, however, specific warrior attitudes that make good sense for the martialist. These warrior attitudes are succinct and definitive.

It may seem that I am repeating the same thing over and over. While it is true that I am doing this, it is only to enforce my teachings upon you. By constant repetition you will soon come to understand my Way of strategy. I will not leave it to you to try to quickly grasp my ideas in passing.

The Book of Five Rings is divided into five sections called Earth, Water, Fire, Wind and No-thing-ness. Earth lays the groundwork for the study of the whole book. Water explains attitudes of warriorness through an understanding of strategy. Fire teaches fighting with the principles of Earth and Water. The Book of the Wind describes the differences between my school's style and the styles of other schools. The Book of No-thing-ness describes the "Way" of nature as the true mode of being.

I have not followed the paths of other men. I have lived without the benefit of a teacher and by my own devices I became the master of myself, and thereby master of the sword and the brush, never differentiating between any of these "arts."

It should be understood that without the assistance of a teacher many roads become open to a practitioner, some on the correct path and some on the incorrect path. It is not for everyone to be without guidance—only a few, and they are exceptional, can make a journey to wisdom without a teacher. You must have extraordinary passion, patience, and self-discipline to make a journey alone. The goals must be understood, definitive, and no diversion can be acknowledged or permitted if you are to attain enlightenment within the sphere of a chosen art. This is a very difficult road to travel and not many are made for it. It is frustrating, confusing, very lonely, certainly frightening, and it will sometimes make you think you do not have much sanity left to deal with the everyday surroundings of your world. Also, there is no guarantee that you will attain perfection. It must all come from inside you without any preconceived notions on your part.

And so we begin....

地

# THE BOOK OF
# EARTH

*N*o man is invincible, and therefore no man can fully understand that which would make him invincible. Even with complete and thorough study there is always the possibility of being defeated and although one may be expert in a particular form, mastery is something a man never stops seeking to attain. It is doubtful that anyone truly understands the "real" way of strategy, much less truly lives it. Yet military leaders must have some understanding of strategy and they must pass it on to their warriors, regardless of the limitations of their own understanding.

There is no one way to salvation, whatever the manner in which a man may proceed. All forms and variations are governed by the eternal intelligence of the Universe that enables a man to approach perfection. It may be in the arts of music and painting or it may be in commerce, law, or medicine. It may be in the study of war or the study of peace. Each is as important as any other. Spiritual enlightenment through religious meditation such as Zen or in any other way is as viable and functional as any "Way." Certainly in the "Way" of the sword or the fist. A person should study as they see fit.

A warrior should have an understanding of the peaceful

arts as well as the killing arts. This is a two-fold Way. If a man chooses a certain Way and seems to have no particular talent for this Way, he can still become a master if he so chooses. By keeping at a particular form of study a man can attain perfection either in this life or the next (if a next life is believed in). The warrior, however, understands that the end result of any study is a kind of death (sublime, not necessarily physical) before the attainment of perfection. Many different types of people have been known to die for either the right reasons or the wrong reasons. The only shame in dying incorrectly is to die a stupid and meaningless death. To die as a warrior means to have crossed swords and either won or lost without any consideration for winning or losing. There is just not enough time and generally there is not enough strength in the resolve of any man to do otherwise.

In all accomplishments of war the warrior understands that the only real measure of his ability lies in being able to beat men in fights regardless of their nature. Failure in any other area is not to be construed as a true test of a warrior's mettle. The true virtue of strategy is in allowing us to overcome all odds in daily life and in helping us attain the closest state we can to being one with the supreme power before going into battle. The development of warrior consciousness is an ongoing thing. Each new experience continually leads to new challenges.

The "Way" cannot be learned through frivolous contests in which the outcome is for the name of a school or a large trophy. It can only be realized where physical death is a reality.

## THE WAY OF STRATEGY

The Way is a specific and determinedly deliberate methodology. The ancient masters must be studied constantly without respite, even when the practitioner thinks he has grasped the knowledge.

It is important to realize that technique is not the end of an art. Those good in technique, regardless of the art they pursue, are not necessarily able to teach the true meaning of an art. Beginning students who do not know this and who think that they are being brought to the threshold of understanding are not to blame so much as those who teach without understanding the inner and the outer worlds of the art of which they profess to be masters. It is useless for people who look good in play competition to think in terms of being masters. They appear to understand and as a result permit their own self-importance to convince them that they are bearers of the truth. Only through a constant search from within, based on one's own lifestyle, can the truth be known. It is absolutely a personal thing. Commercialism does nothing to enhance the reality of truth, although it can lead one to the start of the path.

A man cannot understand the perfection and imperfections of his chosen art if he cannot see the value in other arts. Following rules only permits development up to a point in technique; to advance further the student and artist must learn and seek other knowledge. It makes sense to study other arts as well as those of strategy. Who has not learned something more about themselves by watching the activities of others? To learn the sword, study the guitar. To learn the fist, study commerce. To only study the sword will make you narrow-minded and will keep you from growing outward.

Everything is for sale, including men's souls. A man cannot understand the art he is studying if he only looks for the end result without taking the time to delve deeply into the reasoning of the study. There is no purpose in trying to determine whether one is better than another. If anything is anything, then everything is everything.

Do not confuse profit with profitability. To sell yourself based on the design of your school symbol is unfair to students and is, moreover, moronic because it fools the unknowing into thinking that skill is based on superficiality. Besides, it is bad karma and it will come back to haunt you. You cannot fool with the "spirit of the thing itself." It is a far greater wisdom than man can ever understand.

In our society there are four classes of people. Each fulfills appropriate functions and each is able to attain levels of perfection according to its own means. The specific ranks of the classes in order of their importance to the society are: 1) the Samurai; 2) the farmers; 3) the artisans; and finally, 4) the merchants. Each is respected and disrespected equally by the other classes. The Samurai are warriors and live a "higher ideal." The study of their weapons is their prime motivation. Farmers are next because they provide the food needed for the masses. Artisans are the craftsmen and makers of weapons and other products. Merchants are a ridiculed class because they produce nothing except profit from the work of others. Yet it must be understood that each has a viable and functional part within the structure of the society and that even though, for example, the warrior class may despise the merchant class, we are all too aware of the need for them to maintain the economy. Money must be made to pay the army.

---

## COMPARING THE WAY OF THE CRAFTSMAN TO THE STRATEGY OF A WARRIOR

It is important to understand what the goal of an "art" is. Once that is understood it is easy to pursue the "spirit" of it. To study carpentry you study the correlation of materials and so I can compare the Way of the warrior to the Way of the craftsman. To study the sword you study war, weapons, and men. To study craftsmanship you study the project, the tools, and men. You will succeed or fail in either one depending on your attitude towards the "spirit of the thing." There can be no let up to your study, regardless of the path you choose, even though you may have mastered a particular level. You must search constantly for still more understanding of your chosen art.

If there is no discipline, how can there be a true realization of an ideal? How can a man be trusted to perform in society if he does not understand what society needs? To act in harmony with the environment of where you are you must understand the need for certain rules. If you do not, then you will not be able to control others. If you cannot control others, then how can you expect to attain perfection in your own ideal?

It is essential for the leader to know the rules of the game:

which rules work, which rules do not work, which rules can be changed to suit a particular need, which rules, when changed, will create additional problems, and which will not. Craftsmen are familiar with the quality of the materials they use in their work. A man must not assume that another man's uniform or armament is an indication of his strength. Many warriors have always relied on the "look" of their armor to intimidate the enemy. Do not assume that what appear to be finely crafted goods will hold up under use. The truth is that strength lies in the interior of the warrior: in his heart, his mind, and his spirit. The same applies to weapons. An excellently crafted weapon is incapable of acting of its own accord—it must be wielded. The extent to which a weapon is well crafted is based solely on the ability of the craftsman. The strengths and weaknesses of the materials used must be understood by the craftsman. A merchant, on the other hand, must rely solely on his ability to manipulate others into believing that his goods are the best. That is the Way of the merchant. The farmer knows when his produce is good and when it is inferior. That is the Way of the farmer. The warrior knows in his heart when he is correct in action and when he is issuing false bravado. All men are the same except for their belief in their own selves, regardless of what others may think of them.

The supervisor on a construction job must assign tasks to his men according to their known abilities. Who is good at what specific aspect of the project? Who can lay floors, who can tile the roof, connect the drainage system? Should this not also be true for warriors? The warrior leader must understand himself before he can understand the realities of commanding others to do his bidding, especially when teaching is involved.

Only when each soldier has been observed can the commander know which warrior will be able to perform a specific act. Otherwise, only chaos can result.

The supervisor of a job should circulate among his men to appraise their strengths and weaknesses. He must praise them where they earn praise and admonish them when they do not fulfill the requirements of the job. But he must praise and admonish equally or there will be a loss of morale and the job may not be finished correctly. Likewise, a commander must walk among his men if he is to expect a certain level of performance. If he is unaware of the skills of each warrior, how can he know to whom to assign tasks? The commander must praise and admonish in the same manner. This is a virtue of strategy. Why would a commander want a spearman to join the line of archers?

Even if there is tremendous spirit on the part of the spearman, with no experience with the bow his best efforts can only be mediocre.

## WHAT THE WAY OF STRATEGY IS

A warrior is responsible for his own weapons just as a craftsman is responsible for his own tools. It is simply not possible to get good results without the necessary respect for one's tools or one's weapons. Time must be devoted to training, practicing, and maintaining one's tools or weapons, however gifted a man may be. Each aspect of the craft must be examined over and over again without regard for time and energy spent, whether physically or mentally. The "spirit of the thing" is what will guide a man to his own greatness. There is no Way that can be approached and petitioned for immediate gratification. The Universe does not work that way. How could it and at the same time expect any perfection to develop? If you permit the spirit to permeate your being, the spirit will permeate through you by permitting you to be its instrument. When the warrior becomes skilled and understands his chosen weapons, when he cares for them with a sense of oneness knowing they are used to defeat enemies, he can be self-assured as a warrior. He can then become a commander. A craftsman must likewise understand the spirit of his tools. He must care for them as for his very own self. Only then can he meld with them to become the end product. That is what is meant by the sword being the soul of the samurai.

A warrior must be proficient in all the tools of his trade. He should understand the functions of all weapons and the functions of all military regimentation. A lancer should understand the sword, a kempoist should understand ju-jitsu technique, and a doctor should know carpentry. How else could they meet the unexpected without knowing how the opposition's weapons work? It is also suggested that the warrior familiarize himself with the actual workings of other weapons. In this way a foreign attack will not overwhelm him with its technique, even if it has never been encountered before. Constant study of every aspect of the warrior's craft is essential to understanding the true value of one's particular skills. This is what the ancients meant when they said to think deeply about things. This is another way to grow in your skills. For example, what would your reaction be if you were studying one craft of warriorness and then found that you truly enjoyed working with a different weapon? Contemplate the reality of this. Do not make the mistake of thinking that it is sufficient to finish one section of a job without having planned its continuation. If you are going to construct a desk you must plan for drawers, knobs, etc. If not, the work may appear to be aesthetically pleasing but in reality will be disharmonious with the Universe. Masters plan for contingency even when it appears that they are only improvising. The presentation of an idea, apparently improvised, is only valid if there has been adequate study and preparation on the part of the teacher who can then deliver the information in the proper sequences. A master achieves the Way by being devoted to the art, while the art itself reveals its true identity to a warrior only when the "spirit of the thing itself" feels comfortable with the warrior as a vehicle for its own expression.

If you wish to learn my Way of strategy you must do sufficient research and study. Doing sufficient research means that you must devote yourself as much as possible to the study of these ideas—to the degree with which you feel that you will have accomplished that which you wanted to accomplish. The level of commitment that you give to it will indicate to it what to reveal of itself to you. I knew what I was going to do when I began this book, and my steadfast devotion permitted the "spirit of the thing itself" to produce the results.

## THE MEANING OF THE FIVE PARTS
## OF THIS BOOK OF STRATEGY

The name of this book is Five Rings. Buddhist teachings contain the five elements of the universe. Earth, Water, Fire, Wind and No-thing-ness.

In the Book of Earth the strategy of my school is explained. You are being told the reasons for my writings as well as their structure. You must not depend on understanding your art only by studying the one art with which you are involved. It is difficult to understand the universe if you study only one planet. One must be aware of all of the arts by becoming familiar with many of them as part of one's complete devotion to one of them. Endeavor to know all things. Though you cannot ever do this, you will become more aware of the world around you, an essential strategy if you choose to be a warrior

In the Book of Water I explain that water fills all shapes and eventually wears down any form of captivity. I clearly explain what my Ichi school proposes for the study of strategy. There are many ways of understanding simple things, but generally the opposite is true for difficult ideas.

Study what I say with the desire to understand my Way of strategy. When you have mastered the basics of sword fighting you will be able to beat one man or many men. The result would be the same if you were fighting a countless horde so long as your strength remained with you. The amount of strength you have depends upon the training and practice you have put into your art. It is important to remember that all things can only be built from the ground up and in one stage at a time. Spirit is the thing that must be concentrated upon. To know ten thousand things, know one well. It is difficult to understand these ideas broadly through the use of words. The realities are mostly intuitive. The proper attitude of spirit must be constantly studied. The Book of Water explains the specifics and particulars of my Ichi school.

The Book of Fire is about fighting. When a man fights in real combat his spirit becomes fierce. There is a time for the spirit to be large and a time for the spirit to be small. In order to be able to determine the possible outcomes of combat situations you must constantly maintain the proper attitude by practicing diligently. You can only fight the way you practice. By maintaining the proper attitude, you will always practice diligently with the proper spirit and ensure your ability to become that much stronger. Through practice you will be able to properly maintain yourself at all times.

It is hard to perceive small movements in an enemy but it is easy to see large movements in many men. When studying the art of strategy it is necessary to practice day and night. I cannot stress this enough. You will come to realize what I am saying as the Way to strategy. Your normal life must be a life of strategy. Full combat in battle is explained in this book. Your spirit must remain unchanged as long as you study. As long as you live the warrior life.

The Book of Wind concerns itself with the strategies and teachings of other schools and the traditions of the past. There are obvious differences and there are differences that are not so easy to ascertain. One must be careful not to study traditional methods that diverge from the true teaching of the path. I make the differences very clear and easy to understand. A slight error in judgment while at sea can throw you miles off course. You must constantly study your Way to ensure that you do not lose your way. It is very easy to be side-tracked from the direct method. You must understand what I am talking about when the differences between the Ichi school and others are explained. It is not wrong to think that methods that teach only sword fighting are incorrect, but the advantage of my Ichi school's style of two-sword fighting lies in its mental and physical technique.

To learn technique is essential. However, strategic thinking has its own principles and they can be applied to anything that has to do with war and combat. In this way the Ichi school breaks from traditional teaching.

It is easy to understand the first four books of the Five Rings. Introductory remarks concerning the outline of the five books should be understood upon simple review. Nothing profound is revealed in the introduction. The basic idea of the Way of strategy is the attitude of being or not-being and will be expanded upon. However, in the Book of No-thing-ness you will learn that the Way of strategy is also the Way of nature and that there is no difference except for what we ourselves conceive or misconceive as truth. When you understand the Way of strategy you will be able to hit a man without a thought in a completely natural manner. There is a sound approach to understanding the entire subject. The Book of No-thing-ness is also the shortest of the written tracts, and is at the same time both simple and difficult to comprehend.

## WHY I CALL MY SCHOOL "ONE WAY—TWO SWORDS"

It is common for a warrior to carry two swords. One is a long sword and the other is a short sword. The names for the swords varies from place to place and time to time. My school teaches the proper use of both swords in combat even though a warrior can rely on either one or the other. Spears, lances and bows with arrows are generally used out of doors, as is the sword. Swords are used indoors and outdoors but mainly for close combat. You must be able to wield the swords in any situation. The comparison between halberds, spears, bows and arrows is evident and makes perfect sense in the context of a combat situation. The sword is easier to deal with regardless of the terrain where you happen to be fighting. At the beginning of training, lances, spears, and other weapons are certain to prove difficult, especially if you have never had experience with them. But in time all things work to your advantage when you pursue them with an open heart. I insist that my students start their training with both swords in either hand. In a combat situation you must understand how to make complete use of your weapons. Any other reasoning is foolish. If you are going to die in battle then you should do so with the utmost respectability and dignity. It is a terrible shame to die in battle with your sword undrawn or yourself unable to use it correctly. Because my system employs both swords, a warrior must hold the sword in one hand. It is hard to use a sword correctly when it is held with both hands.

You are also limited to the use of the one sword when the other sword remains passive. A drawn weapon is a killing device and must be used as such. It is not for play. Whatever your determination or will-power, it is foolish to try to change the nature of things. Things work the way they do because that is the Way of things. The warrior should fully understand the nature of the weapon he is using. The long sword is used in a broad manner and the short sword for in-close combat.

Your choice of weapons does not make much difference if you understand their nature. You must also understand the purpose of their existence as well. Once this is done, you will then be able to wield any weapon that you have trained with if you have trained with all your heart. The main idea of my Way of strategy is to win. There is nothing else.

The following is a philosophical truth. One thing does one thing, two things do four things. Think this through. If you are fighting a crowd or controlling a group, it is better to use two swords than one.

It is very hard to explain these ideas in detail because of their intuitive nature. Once you have understood the depth of the thing you are studying, the "spirit" of all things will reveal itself to you.

To master the long sword is to be a master of strategy in my school. As I have mentioned before, the sword has long been called the "soul of the warrior." There is a closeness between the warrior and his weapon. All weapons are warrior's equipment and a part of strategy. When a warrior is master of the long sword, he can rule the world; he can certainly beat ten men or more in combat. To further illustrate my point, consider the unarmed warrior as being even closer to the ideal because no weapon other than "empty hands" is used. To go still further, consider the attitude of "thing-nothing"—an attitude which must not be confused with the concept of "nothing" which is still "something" by definition. The sword is a physical object and is feared by most men, warriors or not.

The craft of the warrior and his Way is the only thing that deals directly with physical living and physical dying. Other arts do not. To understand the Universe one must be in accord with the truths of other matters in order to understand more deeply the conviction needed to pursue the Way of the warrior. Other Ways do not deal with life and death. They deal with ideas that may or may not be acceptable to others. There is a significant difference between beating a man intellectually and physically taking his life. We live in a physical world and are governed much more by the things that can affect us physically than by psychological brow-beating.

## THE ADVANTAGE OF USING
## WEAPONS IN STRATEGY

*E*ach weapon has its own "spirit." Each weapon must be used in its proper place in order to be effective and enable the handler of the weapon to take advantage of its properties. The ultimate weapon is "thing-no-thing." In addition to physical weapons consider the use of "empty hands" to be the ultimate physical weapon. Now consider the use of "empty mind."

You must study with the idea in mind of being able to function in any situation with any weapon. If you study hard and understand the properties of all weapons, they may be used effectively in any situation. Attack weapons like the spear and the bow are good at the onset of an attack but become virtually useless when involved with up-close combat. This does not mean that the bow is entirely useless. Remember to read with understanding and to keep in mind the weapons that are used in warfare. As new weapons are developed they should also be studied with the proper intent of the warrior, which is to master strategy.

The gun is a formidable weapon and has no equal at the beginning of an onslaught but it becomes useless in combat at close quarters because of the difficulty of reloading. The lance and spear must be used at a distance and the bow is of no use in close combat either. Consider the times you are living in and the weapons available to you. As times change and new weapons are made available to you, you must continue to study the nature of these weapons and learn to work with them in learning my strategy.

The weapon is a tool to be used efficiently and effectively; otherwise it will be of little value, even in the hands of a master. With the long sword or with empty hands, the stance should be strong, the cuts, strikes, punches and kicks strong, and the spirit unyielding in the face of battle. This will depend on the amount of heart you have put into your training and practice. Weapons may have decorations on them to enhance the spirit of the warrior but they should primarily be built for durability.

It is dangerous for a warrior to know only one thing. It

will eventually create shortsightedness and limit the possibilities for additional growth. What is the sense of knowing a thing to such a degree that you become oblivious to other things? If you constantly disregard the possibilities of other methods and tools, then you become short-sighted and may in fact lose the advantage of your own strength. That is why the warrior must learn the techniques of other schools and apply that information to the system being studied here.

## WHY TIMING IS IMPORTANT IN STRATEGY

There are good times and there are bad times—for everything. When you understand timing, then you also understand rhythm. Timing and rhythm—they are one and the same thing, yet they are different. To understand them both as one, you must understand them individually. It is absolutely essential to understand the timing of Universal harmony as well. Timing can be altered. Rhythm can be altered. They can be altered individually or in unison. You must understand that in order to restructure time you should have a complete understanding and realization of the universe or else your own substance will be infected with error and you will not be able to perform properly in battles of any type. I cannot stress enough that this comes with constant practice. Understanding timing and rhythm is essential to my strategy. You should always train with timing and rhythm uppermost in your mind, and realize that there are different types of timing and different types of rhythm. Understand them well and you will understand my Way of strategy.

## ENDNOTES TO THE BOOK OF EARTH

*I*t must be understood that training is never completed. When the warrior thinks that training is over he will find that the "spirit of the thing itself" he has been studying will elude him and fail to provide him with any future revelations. He must never stop training. In this way the spirit of the warrior will continue to grow.

The Way of the warrior is a Way of life and can never be construed as a hobby unless you are seeking only to impress others with your technique. You must never stop studying the written passages of masters relating to the art you have chosen to practice. Nor should you stop studying other arts that the warrior studies to broaden his horizons. The heart is essential in helping the intellect to understand the spirit.

If you do not have a map in unfamiliar terrain, how can you hope to get to where you want to go without difficulty? Even if you have directions, you may still have to negotiate roadblocks along the way. Likewise, if you do not set your mind and heart on the required principles, how can you ever hope to understand what it is you are trying to accomplish?

It is important for the warrior to constantly meditate upon these things:

1) Think honestly within yourself in your dealings with all men.

2) Constant training is the only Way to learn strategy.

**3)** Become familiar with every art you come across.

**4)** Understand the Way of other disciplines.

**5)** Know the difference between right and wrong in the matters of men.

**6)** Strive for inner judgment and an understanding of everything.

**7)** See that which cannot be seen.

**8)** Overlook nothing, regardless of its insignificance.

**9)** Do not waste time idling or thinking after you have set your goals.

The nine basic attitudes I have listed are essential for freeing your spirit from negative thoughts that would interfere with your journey. They must be thought about constantly; you must take them into your heart. Once you have accepted the need to study these attitudes, you can proceed with deliberateness, diligence and comfort. You will be able to beat many men just by looking them in the eye. They will realize that you are a formidable opponent and will not have the heart to attack.

Remember timing. Do not forget harmony with the Universe and self. Remember that continuous study is essential for approaching perfection in a chosen art. Although some people may appear to be "there" they too must continually deal with change—based on the rise and fall of timing and rhythm. However, through devotion to the Way of your art you can remove yourself from the general mass of people and be able to concentrate more effectively on your chosen Way.

It is also essential to remember the need to function in society, good or bad, and that in order for your Way to be successful, you must interact with society. If you wish to control others you must first control yourself. That is why it is necessary to study continuously. This is the essence of my strategy.

So ends the Book of Earth.

# THE BOOK OF
# WATER

*I*n the Book of Water the entire strategy of my two-sword school is revealed. You should think each thing through completely and not simply gloss over the words. It is important to understand what you are reading and studying. Should you approach a concept that you do not understand it would be foolish, if you are making the warrior way your life style, to continue on. When I say that language is limited in certain respects it should be understood that while information may be evident, knowledge is not necessarily obvious. There are "hidden" meanings—not to be confused with non-understandable things—that must be thought through constantly until you reach an understanding. When you reread this book you will see another level of understanding come to light. In fact, each time you pick the book up to study it again, you will interpret the teachings differently. This does not mean that your previous understanding was wrong. It simply means that you are proceeding to ask the "spirit of the thing" to reveal itself on a higher level.

While it appears that the rules of strategy are explained here in terms of single combat fights, you should also think on a larger plane to understand battles involving many men.

There is no limit to a man's ability once he understands the strategic principles of an art, for they will also be useful when applied to other situations.

It is important for you to make sure you understand what you are reading. When you study strategy and grasp meanings even slightly incorrectly you will eventually be far off course. When you understand what I am telling you, apply what you have learned to your everyday life.

Imitation is the surest form of flattery and failure. I am not interested with your talk about my ideas. I am more interested in your applying them to your life. If you do not, then you are essentially not in accord with your own mind. This does not apply to those of you who read merely for enjoyment, but only to those who strive to be warriors. Study so as to absorb my teachings into your heart.

## THE IMPORTANCE OF CORRECT SPIRITUAL AND PHYSICAL BEARING IN STRATEGY

The manner in which a warrior carries himself is of the utmost importance both physically and mentally. You are undoubtedly familiar with men who are quiet and strong and seem to be doing nothing.

They do not appear to be tense and do not appear to be in disarray. They simply appear. This is exactly the appearance for which they strive. When it is necessary to attack, they do so with complete resolve, sure of themselves, neither overbearing in attitude nor with false humility. They attack with one purpose and one purpose only—to destroy the enemy.

They do not take false postures when they prepare for attack. They simply attack with all their heart and soul.

A small man can beat a much larger man and one man can beat many men in a fight. Allow your wisdom to develop by constantly striving to perfect yourself in your own art and by understanding the arts of others. When you understand yourself and you understand the enemy you cannot be defeated. Be aware at all times of what is right and wrong among men. Do not permit yourself to be intimidated by the size of the enemy. Do not be fooled by your own misunderstanding of what your purpose is. To do so is wrong thinking and means that you are not studying the principles of my Way properly.

Whether on or off the battlefield, there is no difference in spirit. The warrior sees all of life as the battlefield. Do not lose heart if the enemy's appearance is overwhelming. You must commit yourself to constant study in order to develop the perfection in your soul evident in the demeanor of the spirit.

### HOW YOU SHOULD STAND
### IN COMBAT READINESS

I always stress form and balance. If you are lax in your stances and positioning, then you will be unable to perform your technique effectively. Focus your concentration on only one thing—making the "hit." Narrow your eyes slightly and ever so subtly flare your nostrils. Always fight with your spine erect and unbent. Keep your shoulders relaxed and lowered. Tighten your abdominal muscles and root yourself into the ground. Make yourself bigger in your mind than you are as a manner of intimidating the enemy. Slowly work your way toward the enemy until you are ready to strike. Then do so with utmost conviction, quickness, and power. Keep your weapons ready at all times. You should practice the proper stances and movements prior to using any fighting technique and in this manner establish your own sense of being through your particular art. How often have you witnessed so-called experts with no form or balance? You see them as clods with no style or grace. Think this through and consider how you yourself wish to be seen should the time come for you to move. Think about being seen only by yourself and not through the eyes of others.

Why would you want to appear as one thing and be another? If you are a warrior then you are a warrior and if you are not a warrior then you are not a warrior. The Way of the warrior is the Way of the warrior. To be a warrior, look like a warrior and stand like a warrior. Do not be false to yourself.

## LOOKING AT THE ENEMY

*L*ook at the enemy as if you are looking through him without being too obvious about it. Perception and sight are two important principles in my strategy. Perception relies on intuition. This is developed through practice. Sight is based on the physical ability to use the eyes. Understand the difference and sameness of perception and sight. One must be prepared for the possibility of losing one's sight in mortal combat.

Learn to see things far away and up close. This applies as well to the attitudes towards stance and positioning. Do not prejudge a view according to what you think things should appear to be, but instead look at all things equally and in this way you will be able to discern what can hurt you and what cannot.

Peripheral vision is of the utmost importance. It is a skill that is developed over a period of time in training. This is a stern discipline. It should be used in everyday life as well. I must insist upon training as the means of attaining excellence in the craft of the warrior. Steadfastness of purpose is above all the essential requirement for understanding yourself in relation to the Universe. If you lack this you will be easily led into false securities and will therefore become easy to defeat. Force yourself to develop the skills needed to be the warrior that you define yourself to be. Remember, as you submit to the "spirit of the thing," that the "spirit of the thing" will submit itself to you.

## HOLDING THE LONG SWORD

It is important for you to understand the proper manner in which to hold the long sword. The grip should be both loose and tight at the same time. What I mean by this is that you should hold the sword firmly and resolutely, yet at the same time your hand and wrist must be pliable. Hold the sword as you would a fishing rod and strike with it as if you were casting a fishing line. Hold the sword tightly with the bottom two fingers to give yourself the added support you need to wield the long sword correctly. Direct the sword with your thumb and forefinger.

These principles apply to the unarmed martialist as well. Having some play in your hands is essential in your structured physical attitude, whatever you are trying to accomplish. If you do not hold the sword correctly, you stand a chance of losing control of the weapon when in combat. If you strike a hard object and your grip is not strong, you can drop the sword as a result. In unarmed styles of fighting, the fist must be held tightly and the wrist must be straight. The problems that will occur if you do not do this include breaking your wrist on contact and the inability to focus with all your heart and soul with a weakened wrist. In knife-hand techniques, the fingers must be drawn tightly together to prevent the breaking of the fingers if your strike is not focused correctly. If your fingers are drawn tightly together, you will have no problems with focusing.

When a warrior draws his sword the main intention must be to cut the enemy down. There is no reason to change your grip when you strike the enemy. When you have forced the enemy to lose control of his sword because of your parrying thrust, do not change your hand position. Do not show your enemy false bravado because it is certain to get you killed, especially if the enemy is well trained. Likewise, when you put aside the enemy's sword, or block the enemy's strike, you must be intent on following up with a powerful attack to win the fight. The martial arts are not a game to see who is stronger and who is faster. You must mean it when you strike at the enemy. If you do not, you will certainly get hurt. The only reason to draw your sword is to cut the enemy down. It is essential that you understand there is no difference between using the sword in combat and in practice. There is no such thing as a grip for striking and a grip for practice. Even in practice you must strike with all your heart and with all your soul. To do otherwise will result in your being unable to strike with full force and conviction should the need arise. Every strike must be done with full authority and full intensity. A bullet from a gun does not make a distinction between practice and combat. You are training to be one and the same way in your entire life. I do not like the idea of stubbornness in the grip. Stubbornness means non-flexibility. Your hands must be both pliable and firm. This means that you must practice all techniques in the same manner, regardless of which way you hold your sword in swordfighting or your hand in unarmed methods.

## UNDERSTANDING THE MOVEMENT OF YOUR BODY THROUGH PROPER FOOTWORK

There is no difference between walking and running into battle or walking and running in everyday life except for speed. Proper movement of the body depends entirely on the manner in which you carry yourself. The feet carry the body and the body directs the feet. Tread firmly with the heel touching the ground first and then roll forward to the ball of your foot. Practice this until you appear to move without motion. Do not use different types of steps such as jumping, gliding or hopping. Combat is an aspect of your every-day life if you follow the path of the warrior. Do not allow for differences in your attitude. Refer back to the discussion on stances and positions. "Special" types of movements are used specifically for special techniques and are not to be cultivated to form your being-in-motion. Walking is walking, whether in an excursion to the park or in a combat maneuver.

The ancients tell us to walk in the manner of Yin and Yang. Even when you step forward, backward, or sideways with one foot, the other foot is not to be considered apart from the whole. When you attack right foot forward or when you attack left foot forward, the idea is to move the body and not just the feet. The incorrect way of moving the feet will eventually trip you up and make you lose your balance. This is bad for the warrior, as it causes a loss of poise. You should practice all techniques from both sides of the body. In this way you will not become used to functioning from only one direction. To do so is foolish and diminishes your abilities. Do not be a "righty" or a "lefty." Become both by practicing your movements from all directions.

## THE FIVE POSITIONS OF ATTACK

If we consider the possibilities for attacking the enemy we can clearly see that there are only five ways to do so. You attack the upper, middle, lower, right, and left sides only. This does not exclude attacking from behind the enemy's back. I am talking about attacking. You should understand the reason for this. You can only attack the upper, middle, lower, right, or left side of the body. Front or rear goes without saying—it is still upper, middle, lower, right, or left side. Even though this may seem ridiculous to mention, there are those who will seek to attack in a completely disjointed fashion when coming from the rear, and thereby fail to beat an enemy. Nothing fancy is involved. You go straight to the heart of the matter and defeat the enemy. These is nothing else involved. You either do it or you don't. There is only one purpose in attacking the enemy—to cut him down with finality.

Go straight into the heart of the enemy. Your main purpose as a warrior is to defeat the enemy. Do not be side-tracked by the appearances of the enemy or yourself. Do not be conscious of the particular technique you will use. This causes hesitation. If you understand this mentality, you will never be beaten. Your attitude will be recognized by potential enemies and they will prefer to fight someone else. The ultimate aim of the martial arts is not having to use them.

It is always best to attack straight ahead. Your attack must be filled with conviction and purpose. In this way you defeat the enemy regardless of his abilities. Straight-ahead attacks are decisive. This does not mean that straight-in attacks have no circular movements. Research this well. Depending upon where you are fighting, you must understand when to use a front attack and when to use a side attack. It should not be a conscious decision in combat. This is why you must constantly practice from all sides. Going to the side means that you are encountering some sort of obstruction, perhaps another weapon, a strong attacking force, or something else.

Everything emanates from a central core. This is true of

all things regardless of their appearance. That is why it is said that you emphasize everything you do from the middle of your heart. An attack of any kind must originate from the center of the warrior and go directly to the center of the enemy. It is important to understand the need for concentrating your attack on the middle and letting it take its own course by going up, down, left or right according to the needs of the "spirit of the thing itself." If we observe a large battle arena, we generally see the commander in the middle of the troops. All the other positions surround him. He can therefore direct things accordingly, see clearly, and defeat the enemy with the appropriate strategy.

## UNDERSTANDING THE NATURE OF THE LONG SWORD

In order to be able to fight well you must understand how to handle your weapons, whether they be swords or fists. Constant practice and becoming one with your sword are essential. Even if you should pick up a different weapon, by knowing the heart and nature of your own weapon you will be able to defeat men because of your sensitivity to the one. You must understand the limitations of what you are using before you can use them well. Think about this. It will become obvious in time.

Regardless of combat circumstances, you must always remain calm. Calmness is attained through meditation and belief in your own skills. It is not to be confused with egotistical technique, which generally fails under intense combat situations. Do not try to use techniques that do not fit the situation. An attack must be executed with quickness, not speed. Attack with power, not strength. There is a great difference between speed and quickness, power and strength. Think this through very carefully. It is the essence of strategy. You can use alternate devices as weapons, but their properties must be known or they might fail in a fight. A punch is a punch, a kick is a kick, and a strike is a strike. Do not confuse them with each other, as many often do when trying to use a kick technique where a punch is needed. A long punch is ineffective if used as a jab, and likewise, a jab is ineffective if used like a lunge punch. Understand the properties of the long sword and the short sword. Understand your weapons.

Always return your weapon along the same path it traveled out on. In this way you can use it again without having to relocate and rethink your attitude. The same applies to bringing the opposite hand back to the hip when you execute a punching strike. You must do this with authority and not in a haphazard manner. To fire a powerful punch requires that you fire straight and true while at the same time bringing the other hand back into a firing mode. Otherwise both movements will be weak.

## THE FIVE APPROACHES

I must insist that you understand the need for constant training with the correct attitudes in order to wield a sword properly. The Way of the warrior is an exacting Way and the "spirit of the thing itself" will not be trifled with. You must understand my five approaches to strategy.

The best way to attack is to the center of the enemy. Always go to the middle of the enemy's face. It is easier to veer off in another direction from the center then it is to cover excessive ground in getting from the right side to the left side or the left side to the right side. When you attack you generally have to ward off an attack at the same time. This is called deflection. It is not the same as striking at the enemy's weapon. This is an entirely different matter. In blocking you are trying to ward off an attack. Striking at the enemy's weapon misdirects the enemy's attack in order to open a target for yourself. Riding the enemy's weapon means the same thing.

Your attack must be based on both parts of this maneuver. Neither one nor the other but both. If it is not, then it is not an attack done with conviction and will not be effective. Being directly in the enemy's face is the same thing as pointing your sword into the enemies face. Your directness is what will enable you to succeed.

The upper attack is the second of my attacking strategies. An attack must be made with the idea of repeating it. It is not always possible to cut the enemy or hit the enemy with only one attack. You must not permit confusion to get in the way of your work. Do your work well and do it effectively. When you have come to see that technique is the basis for allowing the spirit to express itself then you can beat the enemy. Always be aware of the possibility of changing timing and rhythm.

The lower attack is done as if arising from the earth. Hit the enemy's hand from underneath his sword position. It is the same as kicking an unarmed fighter in the groin while he is in an attacking position. If your attack is acted upon by the enemy, change direction and come in from the side. The main idea is to move on the enemy instantly upon perceiving his own approaching attack. Superlative speed is essential to be able to move on the enemy at the instant of his attack. Speed does not necessarily mean being faster than the enemy. It means being smarter than the enemy. Think in terms of "quickness." An enemy will attack only if he feels sure of himself. This is why it is important to develop perception. Knowing the enemy will attack does not give you the license to only fight with a counter-attacking attitude. You must have the courage to go into the attack without thinking in terms of anything but "cutting" or "striking" the enemy. Always maintain the attitude of defeating your enemy with one strike. Practice your attacks with the attitude of "going in." The long sword means that you use your primary weapon, yourself.

Attacking from the left side is the fourth approach. Parry from the outside and attack from the left side. You may also attack from the right side. The left side attitude is a method of combat and not a specific technique. Deflect the advancing sword by going into the attack and the instant you touch his sword swing your sword up and across and down.

The fifth approach is to attack from the right side of the enemy. Use the same manner as with the left side attitude, for this is neither more nor less important than any of the other approaches. A methodology is employed, not a specific technique.

Words are not adequate to fully explain what I mean with regard to my five approaches to strategy. The concepts are intuitive. You must constantly practice all of your techniques until they become second nature. Once they are part of your nature you can cease to think about them. You must understand yourself and you must understand the enemy. In the later sections, specific attitudes and ideals are discussed more fully. You would also do well to remember that what I say and how you perceive what I say can be completely different depending upon your awareness of yourself and the level of skill you have attained. The need for constant study and thought is essential for understanding the Way of the warrior.

## THE STRATEGY OF "ATTACK-NO-ATTACK"

It does not matter which of the five attitudes you use because in every situation you must be flexible enough to change the entire structure of your attack—the main purpose being that of cutting or striking the enemy dead. You must wield your sword properly. Be prepared in spirit to change the direction of your attack at any moment. In practice, attack to the upper and in mid-attack immediately

THE BOOK OF WATER

change direction to a lower attack. Attack from the left side and immediately change your attack to a direct middle thrust. Change direction from the right side to a lower attack to an immediate left-sided attack. Constantly experiment and train yourself to understand the changes of my "Attack-No-Attack" strategy.

It is absolutely essential that you understand what is being said here. You cannot take a certain attitude and depend upon it entirely. There are too many variations in attacks from the enemy. What you may think is effective may in fact be ineffective because of the way in which the enemy is "feeling" at that particular moment. Your attitude must be such that you can shift into any other mode of combat without having to make a conscious decision. You must be flexible and you must have no particular liking for any particular set of techniques. Think this through very carefully. It is the basis of the warrior's Way.

A warrior has only one objective—to destroy the enemy by whatever means necessary. If you do not understand this teaching then how can you ever hope to do what you are trying to accomplish? You must go into combat with the attitude of absolutely destroying the enemy. If you do not develop this attitude, what are you doing there in the first place? Combat fighting is not done for fun. Even in practice sessions you must have the attitude of going in for the kill.

Remember, the main idea behind becoming a warrior is learning how to destroy the enemy. Without destroying the enemy you are playing a child's game. Destroy the enemy at any cost even if it means that you yourself may possibly be hurt in the exchange. Think of nothing but of cutting the enemy down. Even when large armies go into battle, their main attitude must be to destroy the enemy, otherwise they will lose and be disgraced. There is no other reason to be a warrior.

---

## BECOMING ONE WITH HITTING THE ENEMY

Perception and intuition are essential in the attitude of destroying the enemy. You must train hard to be able to move into the attack and stop it before it even occurs. This takes great courage. It takes dedication to the art you are practicing. You cannot hope to attain perfection if you cannot go into the attack and destroy the enemy by becoming one with the attack. You must attack as quickly and directly as possible. You must be able to strike the enemy even should he go into a retreat posture. You must continue on, you must not hesitate, and you must be relentless in your conviction. This takes great effort in training and meditation, but it must be done.

You must continue in with your attack regardless of the attitude of the enemy. It is hard to understand this without actual practice and more practice. You must have a "trainer" assisting you in your practice, but if you don't then you must firmly develop the concreteness of the idea into your own mind and body and practice with all your heart and soul. Your attack must be relentless. And it must not be thought of as a thing in itself.

## NO THOUGHT, NO IDEA

There is no need to wait for the enemy to start combat. You go into the attack and if the enemy decides to go in at the same time then you must be quicker, more focused, and more resolved. It is essential that you go into the attack with your body leading your hands and feet. You achieve this by having a more determined attitude and a stronger spirit. Have no preconceived ideas about how a situation should come out. Go into the attack with the attitude of destroying the enemy and you surely will if your spirit is up to the occasion and your heart is into the matter and you do not fear the possibility of being hurt in the exchange. Press in hard with your body, shout with force and authority, and let your hands come from nowhere to destroy the enemy.

## ATTACKING THROUGH THE ENEMY

When you are in a situation where neither you nor the enemy seem able to make the opening needed for the kill, you must summon more resoluteness from within yourself to explode into the enemy's face and body, again leaping in with quickness and deliberateness. Think only of destroying the enemy by any means necessary.

## COMBINATIONS OF ATTACK

W hen you clash with another warrior, and there is no release of conviction on either part, you must employ a diversion in your attack. Strike high, low, and middle using whatever means are necessary to finish off the opponent. You must learn different combinations and techniques down to your soul and they must come without thinking. In unarmed forms of fighting, you attack with punches, kicks, and strikes in rapid succession without pause. Each and every attack you make must be done with full force and authority. You cannot attack half-heartedly. When you finish with one technique, you must immediately continue on with yet another and another until you have attained your goal, which is to destroy the enemy.

## THE FLAME AND FLASH CUT

Y ou must attack with intense focus. You cannot waste time or movement. When both swords come together, your flame must be resolved to penetrate in a flash with utmost intensity. You can never waiver with the intent of your attack. Go in deeply with your body. Not doing so will permit your enemy to find an opening and perhaps destroy you. This you do not want. Go in to the attack with everything you have and then, if necessary, regroup and do it again.

## THE FALLING LEAVES CUT

Falling leaves means that you drop into the enemy with subtle but overwhelming strategy. Falling on the enemy is attacking without preconceived ideas as to how to conclude the battle. In this way you will gain control over the enemy's sword. It is essential that you practice and develop powerful deflection and parrying techniques. Strive to control your enemy's sword. Without practiced deflection and parrying, you are left only with the possibility of having to constantly get around the enemy.

The importance of deflection and parrying techniques cannot be stressed enough. Put as much emphasis into your deflection technique as you put into your parrying technique and turn the attitude of blocking into one of attacking. In this manner you will certainly be able to disable the enemy with only blocks.

## THE SWORD AS AN EXTENSION OF THE BODY

The whole idea in combat is to hit the enemy and destroy him. You absolutely must learn to attack with your whole body using the sword as an extension, just as the arms and legs are extensions of the body. When you attack with your whole being there is little room left for thinking about overprotecting certain areas. You are committed to the attack and you are not concerned about the possibility of getting hurt in retaliation. There are times when you must compress your spirit prior to exploding and times when you must explode before compressing. This is called the Yin-Yang attack. There is no one way to attack and destroy the enemy. Use combinations, single attacks, multiple attacks, etc., with all the tools of your craft such as punching, kicking, and striking. Destroy the enemy by any and all means.

## DIFFERENCES IN CUTTING AND SLASHING ATTACKS

You must be utterly resolved to cut the enemy down. Slashing can be equated with just tapping the enemy with either a sword or a fist. It is not a truly resolved and committed attack. Cutting means that you are firmly resolved to destroy the enemy in one move. This is urgently important to understand. Regardless of the intent of the enemy, you must fire with full force and authority. If you do not, then the opponent will see you as weak and perhaps have no difficulty in cutting you. Cutting is proper form and understanding. Slashing is based on a lack of skill and little belief in your own skills.

## THE BASHFUL MONKEY'S BODY

The Bashful Monkey does not reach out with his arms. There is no spirit in the intention of the attack and it is usually used by those who do not understand the strategy of an attack. The Bashful Monkey is unsure of himself and is probably thinking of the possibility of being hurt. By keeping yourself at more than arm's distance from the enemy, you are essentially not being sure of your own abilities.

The attitude of destroying the enemy with one cut is based on the attitude of "going in" to the attack. If not, your spirit is lacking and your resolve is less than complete. You must always close in on the enemy regardless of the indications of the enemy's strength.

## STICKING TO THE ENEMY LIKE GLUE

Sticking to the enemy like glue means not permitting a gap to grow between yourself and the enemy in combat. You are committed to the attack and should the enemy retreat you must continue on with your attack, making sure that you have cut him down. Not to do so is to practice hesitation; hesitating even for an instant allows the enemy to turn against you again, and possibly defeat you. If you do not stick to the enemy like glue, you are insecure in your convictions. You must develop your spirit to be able to drive right through the enemy without worrying about whether or not you will be hit in return. When you lead with your head and let your body lag, you are effectively throwing your balance off and giving the enemy a target at which to fire. You must drive with your spirit because when you do so your head, legs, and body will move as one.

## MAKING YOURSELF BIGGER THAN YOU ARE

This is a strong warrior attitude. Extend your spirit above and beyond the enemy's body and spirit. Never cringe in fear and never fight without your spine being straight. This indicates your resoluteness to go in hard and deep to cut the enemy down. You first beat the enemy with your spirit and then you beat the enemy with your hands or your sword. Stretch out your body and your spirit. Go for the kill with utter resolve and commitment.

## BEING TENACIOUS IN YOUR BEARING

Stay with the enemy and do not allow him to force any distance between you, for this generally gives the enemy room to maneuver and a chance to bring about a successful counter-strike against you. Do not permit yourself to lose your composure. Do not permit the enemy to separate from you. Do not permit yourself to grapple with the enemy, for this becomes a contest of strength and may prevent you from performing with conviction to slay the enemy with one stroke.

## STRIKING DEEP WITH THE BODY

Striking deep with the body means penetrating right into the enemy's face with full resolve and commitment. When you use your body to penetrate you may be able to knock the enemy off balance, enabling you to continue in with your attack. You should understand the need to be able to "blast" the enemy's body away from his center of balance. You do this the way it is explained. You drive your spirit through the enemy's spirit, using the enemy's body by driving in with your shoulder and focusing your strike against the enemy's very being. You must focus intently and when you have moved the enemy out of position you absolutely must fire with authority, killing the enemy with a single and perfectly executed stroke.

## THREE WAYS TO STRATEGICALLY COUNTER AN ATTACK

My three methods of countering an attack apply to sword fighting as well as unarmed combat. One method is to block an attack by diverting the enemy's sword and continuing to attack right into the enemy's eyes. Another is to sidestep and feint to the side while firing a strike to the other side of the body. A third method is to feign a thrust and drive straight in to the enemy's face with a powerful attack. You must attack with the attitude of cutting rather than slashing. It is quite acceptable to attack the enemy with your bare hand in combination with the sword. In any event, you must always close in on the enemy and not give him a chance to counter against you.

## STABBING AT THE FACE

**W**hen you are aiming for the face the enemy will know it and possibly look to protect the area with a number of different techniques. It is at the very second you see him move that you must charge in with a substantial attack to the body or even to the face. You can approach any area of the enemy's body when he shows any sign of hesitation. What is important is that you continue your attack regardless of where you actually hit him. Aiming for one spot and having your sword make the hit in another spot is something that you will have to develop through constant practice.

## STABBING AT THE HEART

**I**n fighting it is always best to go straight in. Always go straight in, with utter resolve, regardless of the situation. You must not waver when you are making the attack. Doing so will give the enemy the opportunity to go around your attack and beat you. There are times when you will have to use other methods to destroy the enemy, such as coming in from the left side or the right side, or from the upper, middle or lower approaches, but in most situations it is best to go straight in. Think about this as you visualize your methodology.

## TO HUMILIATE THE ENEMY BY BLOCKING AND COUNTERING

*I*n real combat there are usually many blows thrown by each of the combatants. It is truly rare for a fight to consist of one man attacking and the other countering. You must practice constantly to understand the need to continuously strike and counter-strike until your will overcomes the will of the enemy. It is essential that you be able to fire a death strike as a natural extension of your block. You will be able to develop this concept through the repetitive practice of your formal exercises. You must practice with the intensity of real life situations or it becomes a game and you can easily be beaten.

## THE SLAPPING AWAY COUNTER ATTACK

*I*t is important to understand rhythm when you are in combat. The importance of following the enemy's motions and his manner of preparing to attack is crucial to understanding the difference between beating him and being beaten. The idea is to use the enemy's attack as a springboard for your own quick cut attack. You must understand rhythm as an essential part of timing. When you have your timing down, you can become unbeatable because your attack cannot be made to waver even a little. You must think of the entire action as one motion and not two separate moves consisting of a block and a counter. Think this through thoroughly and understand what an attack really is.

## ENEMIES CONTINUE TO COME

This is a very important lesson. When you are fighting more than one enemy you must use both of your swords and strike quickly and strongly without hesitation. You must go for the strongest attacker first, regardless of the appearances of the others. With practice you will understand how to recognize the strongest attacker.

You must constantly move around the fighting area and make sure to befuddle the "gang" by constantly moving into them and keeping them to one side. You must constantly chase them and not permit them to surround you. They are generally not prepared for this type of retaliation and you will have them under your control if you remember to maintain your spirit and destroy them one after another in a consistent fashion. You must continue to fire at them until they are all down and you are certain that they cannot regroup for another attack. If you fail to do this and come under their influence, you will surely be beaten. You must never let this happen. There are more than one against you and you must even the sides as quickly as possible. Therefore, strive to practice with the idea of moving from one technique directly into the rest without hesitation. Practice correct breathing so you are able to maintain the stamina you need. By constantly moving around you give them little choice in their space to fight and they can be controlled and taken out in quick succession. You must also fight with the attitude of no-mind. Do not think of possible outcomes until you have finished with your battle. To do so is foolish and takes your mind off the primary objective, which is to destroy the enemy. Think only of destroying the enemy and the technique will flow of itself.

## TAKING THE ADVANTAGE IN COMBAT

Practice is the only way that you will ever come to understand what the Way of the warrior is about. Constant striving for perfection of the self through a chosen art is the only path to enlightenment. Words can only bring you to the foot of the path, and to attain mastery and perfection you must constantly strive to better yourself through an understanding of your chosen Way.

## ONE ATTACK ONLY

Contemplate winning all your victories with only one strike. You must understand that the reason for your one strike is to slay the enemy. The obvious answer to all things is practice and more practice.

The more you practice, the more the "spirit of the thing itself" will reveal itself to you. For whatever reason you have chosen to be a warrior, you must understand your responsibility to the art and to yourself. They are one and the same.

―――

## UNDERSTANDING THE SPIRIT OF ONENESS WITH YOURSELF AND YOUR SWORD

*T*he entire purpose of my Water Book is to teach you how to become a warrior by using my method of strategy. It is important that you understand each line in it. This is the true basis for learning the Way of the warrior, for by doing so you are also practicing strategy. Carefully learn the five approaches and the five strategies for combat. These principles of strategy work whether you are fighting one man or twenty men. Carefully study rhythm and timing. Strategy is the same in all cases. Remember that you must kill the enemy correctly. Not doing so is not the Way of the warrior. Continue to study my strategy and in time you will certainly understand what it is truly about and it will become a part of your very being. It will become your spirit.

*T*his ends the Book of Water.

# The Book of

# FIRE

The Book of Fire describes the importance of knowing the difference between using a bamboo practice sword and a real sword in combat. Although technique is extremely important and must never be overlooked, there is a tendency among most would-be warriors to concentrate only on the development of their craft through skills developed with certain moves. Would-be warriors who use only the raiment of their profession and brag through their motions do not understand strategy. They overlook the all-important aspect of spirit, thinking that it will come to them without additional work. To release the spirit one must accentuate the work with meditations of the heart and the soul. Not doing so is the same as performing music note for note, with no emphasis on the "feeling" of the particular piece being performed. And so most warriors only perform tricks. The Way of the warrior is filled with soul and feeling. Without it the warrior is essentially "dead" even though he may appear to be very strong.

The only way you can understand the truth about killing an enemy in combat is by killing an enemy in combat. Because this may be difficult to do whenever you may want to, proper practice is essential. Only by studying actual tactics and being able to determine an enemy's strength can you actually understand the meaning of life and death in war. You must train constantly with the attitude of killing the enemy. When this attitude is fully developed, potential enemies will not wish to enter into combat with a warrior they sense has the resolve and conviction of one with no concern for the enemy's well-being. In general, they cannot know the truth of the matter. It is foolish to get into scuffles with an enemy and not attack with a killing resolve. In order to understand life and death, you must actually be in a situation where the possibility of death exists. There is a constant need to study one's weaponry and the methods to be used when real combat occurs. Regardless of this, you must strive for this perfection of your soul by thinking in terms of actually killing enemies when you are practicing.

Through constant application of your training skills, you will come to understand the value of a particular technique if you practice with full resolve and use the methods of visualization in your training. You should practice wearing your full suit of armor in order to learn the true feeling of combat. You can become a master of strategy through thorough and constant practice. By seeing into a particular technique you will learn where and when it can best be used, even though you are not using it for a real purpose at the time.

Training enables you to see deeply into the motivations for your warriorness as well as into the development of your abilities. In this way you learn your craft.

Anyone who truly wishes to master strategy can master strategy. Through constant practice, you become free from your own ideas of what and how things should work. When you learn a technique and apply your "soul" to it you will find that the technique will reveal to you the manner in which it must be used to your personal advantage. This applies to combat without weapons as well. In your everyday dealings with men you will find a special ability that enables you to control situations and maintain your own position without having to submit yourself to the whims of another. However, it should be pointed out that you yourself must have the courage of your convictions and the courage to act on your convictions. Without this "courage" and the ability to "act," you will become another man's pawn and can easily be defeated. This is the only way to learn my principles of strategy. Through constant training, you will eventually be seen as a man of incredible spiritual power.

---

## THE PLACE FROM WHICH YOU FIGHT

*U*se everything to your advantage at all times. In outdoor fights, try to keep the sun behind you. In that way, you maintain an advantage by diminishing the opponents' capacities for sight and perception. When fighting indoors, keep a door or avenue of escape behind you. Sometimes you will be overwhelmed and must have an escape route. Always be in a position where you can look down upon the enemy. In real unarmed situations, you may keep any area free to allow you the possibility of escape if necessary. There is nothing wrong with escaping from combat if you are overpowered and honestly cannot win the fight. Get out and make sure you have provided a means to get out. Seek out the place of advantage whenever you enter into a new area. The same applies to seating arrangements around a table. Always seek to occupy the seat with the most advantage. He who has proper position controls the situation. If it is unavailable to you then get as close to it as you can, either on the left or right, depending upon how your perceptions direct you.

Whether fighting an enemy armed or unarmed, keep him on the defensive. Chase the enemy with your body and your spirit. This is excellent strategy. You can easily open targets for yourself with a little effort, but then you must have the courage to go in and kill the enemy without delay. You must be totally resolved when you are fighting; otherwise you will easily lose. By constantly creating difficulties for the enemy, you will force him to deal with more than one thing, giving you the advantage in killing him swiftly.

When you have the enemy in an awkward position, do not let him regain his composure and possibly defeat you. When the enemy is confused, you must go in for the kill. This strategy must be constantly studied.

## THREE STRATEGIES TO CONTROL THE ENEMY

The best way is to commence with your attack and in this way keep him off balance and on the defensive. The second way is to step back from his attack and draw him to you. The third way is, when you both attack together, to be stronger in spirit. There is nothing else besides these three methods. You either take the lead, hold him off and then take the lead, or force the lead at any given time. This is truly the essence of fighting. Utter resolve is necessary when you are fighting an enemy. In order to beat him you must control the situation, regardless of the method you use. If you do not control the enemy, the enemy will control you.

## THE FIRST CONTROL OF THE ENEMY

By keeping the pressure on the enemy, you will keep him constantly in a defensive posture. It is essential that you remain calm when initiating an attack. Your basic attitude should be of wanting to overwhelm him and unsettle his spirit. This will permit you to control the situation and make good your attack, the purpose of which is to destroy the enemy. You may appear strong and then deliver your cut through guile. It does not matter how you do it as long as you understand why you are doing it. Change your rhythm and change your timing if necessary. You may appear unresolved, but when you approach the enemy you must charge in with utter calm and purpose. You may wish to send the enemy a message implying your superior strength; when the enemy realizes his position, quickly go in for the kill. There are times when, although you are prepared to go right through the enemy, you lay back momentarily and then, without warning, leap in and through.

## THE SECOND CONTROL OF THE ENEMY

D o not let the enemy overwhelm you with his apparent strength and technique. You must remain calm at all times; in this way you can control the attack. When the attack comes, be sure to "misdirect" the aim of the enemy. As an example, feint left and strike from the right. The other way is to sense the attack and, at the very moment of the enemy's movement, charge in with greater strength, power, and resolve.

## THE THIRD CONTROL OF THE ENEMY

N ever be overwhelmed by the enemy. You can ensure this by keeping your spirit tall and your resolve strong. Regardless of how the enemy approaches, your main thought should be to cut him down. Should the enemy attack strongly and calmly, you must become one with the attack, and through superior resolve cut him down swiftly.

Without constant practice, it is hard for words to convey the true meaning of the thought. To come to understand something that appears obvious, you must constantly probe into the meaning of the words. You must unceasingly practice the techniques. When you think you understand something, you have made only the first approach to it. To further clarify your understanding, you must read and read again. Each time you read and practice a "thing," the "spirit of the thing itself" will reveal more of itself to you. Study is a life-long undertaking. That is why it is said that "the warrior first understands being a warrior when he no longer concerns himself with being a warrior." The main thing to understand is that you must have no hesitation in killing the enemy.

## TO SUFFOCATE THE ENEMY WITH A PILLOW

What is meant by suffocating the enemy with a pillow is never permitting him to gain an advantage over you in any way. You can be sure the enemy is thinking likewise; either you lead the enemy or he will lead you. You must come to understand the value in this concept. You must also understand that the reason an enemy is fighting you is because the enemy thinks that he will defeat you. You must react instantly to an enemy's attack. This can only be accomplished after thorough and diligent practice. If you understand this principle, then you will be able to sense an impending attack and react properly by killing the enemy before he kills you. The main thrust of my entire teaching is training and contemplation on the Way of the warrior; it is the only thing that should be in your life. It may appear that there is no room for anything else, but the reverse is true. When you are committed to a particular thing, everything else falls into place because you are not permitting yourself to be side-tracked by anothers' whims. The strength of your courage to act on your convictions is most important in this regard. It is very hard to devote your life to something and not have anything else appear that provides you with the simple pleasures of life. On the other hand, if you pursue your perfection through a particular Way, then that will give you the pleasure of the "spirit of the thing itself." These things are hard to understand when only written in words.

You must follow through with hard study, hard practice and immense belief in your own ideal. You have chosen to be a warrior for your own reasons. Regardless of the Way you have chosen, if you truly believe in the principles of what you are doing, you will be able to attain perfection. It does not come overnight. When you understand this, you will be a master of strategy.

## CROSSING THE RAVINE

Having the courage to enter into combat when the time and place are right is what I mean by crossing the ravine. It is essential to have the courage of your convictions and the courage to act upon them. This is the strategy of crossing the ravine. If you are always aware of your surroundings, then you will always be able to cross at the correct time. However, men are not perfect in any aspect of their lives, no matter the amount of time, effort, and energy they put into their search for perfection. The virtue of perfection is that it is always just beyond a man's reach. This is good. If perfection were attainable then it would have no value— there would be no reason to pursue it. In this light, always know the strengths and weaknesses of yourself and your enemy. Always be aware of the easiest way to accomplish something. Do not strive to do something difficult because you seek favor in the eyes of others.

## KNOWING THE RIGHT TIME

*H*ow do you feel about going into combat? Is your spirit correct at all times? Are you feeling strong? Do you feel slightly uneasy? It is important that you understand yourself with regard to the possibility of fighting. Another consideration is that the enemy has these thoughts as well. The better you know the opponent, the better equipped you are for battle. The skill you need to win a battle lies in knowing the enemy's strengths and weaknesses. You achieve this through constantly practicing with the attitude of destroying the enemy, knowing where you are at all times, and understanding your relationship to the battle. Knowing the time means that you can instantly assess a situation and act accordingly. When you have acquired the correct attitude, you will be able to easily beat the enemy because you will be truly prepared to go into combat with an understanding of all the skills and abilities that you and your opponent possess.

## TO STEP ON THE ENEMY'S SWORD

*I*t is difficult to attack the enemy if you are busy preparing your weapons for combat. You must come to understand the importance of attacking while the enemy is attacking and, in doing so, step on his sword, making him lose balance and advantage. You must go directly into the attack and beat the enemy before the enemy has the chance to realize what is happening. This is the classic strategy of "misdirection." Would you not want the enemy to stop and think about what he was doing when he starts to attack? Of course you would, and therefore it is foolish not to think that the reverse is true. As soon as you sense the possibility of an attack, you must react immediately with your own attack to kill the enemy or you will give him the chance to regather himself and come at you again. You absolutely must commit yourself to overwhelming the enemy by instantly retaliating against him. While the enemy is attempting to attack you and you have the attitude of stepping on him, you can belittle the enemy when you see his strengths and weaknesses. You must step on him with your body and your spirit and continue on to win the fight by killing him.

## COLLAPSING THE ENEMY'S SPIRIT

Depending upon the amount of conviction you have in regard to the enemy, you can easily get him to collapse under the pressure of your attack. You do this by forcing him to make unnecessary moves, thereby throwing off his timing and rhythm. Once you have made it necessary for the enemy to regather himself, he is at his most vulnerable. It is at this moment that you immediately go for the kill with nothing else on your mind except destroying the enemy. Go after the enemy with a resolute spirit. You must stay after the enemy or he will have a chance to reposition himself, possibly making an even stronger second attack. When you go for the kill, go for the kill. Do not relinquish your position through any weakness on your part. To do so is deadly and will cost you the battle.

---

## BECOMING THE ENEMY

D enigrate the enemy constantly and with great spirit. Do not acknowledge the possibility that the enemy is stronger than you are. Do not accept the possibility that the enemy is smarter than you are in any way whatsoever. If you are aware of the Way of the warrior, you are aware of the Way of the warrior. The Way of the warrior does not permit you to accept an inferior position to anything.

You are either the best or you are not the best. If you are, then you will win; if you are not, then you will lose. There is nothing to argue about here. You must also remember your level of understanding. This falls into the area of knowing yourself as well as knowing the enemy. To become the enemy, see yourself as the enemy of your enemy. If you understand strategy, you will know how to beat the enemy. Think this over until it is clear in your mind.

---

## TO RELEASE THE GRIP OF FOUR HANDS

W hen you and the enemy are of equal spirit and skill and neither of you can get the other to move, there is a standoff. This can result in deadly consequences. It is called the grip of four hands. It is foolish to stand there toe to toe and not be able to get the job done, which is to kill the enemy. If an impasse occurs, sneak something else into the combat and win decisively. Combat must never be a thing of pride or stubbornness. If you must change your method of attack, do so without hesitation. Change your timing, change your rhythm, change your approach. It does not matter who is stronger or who is faster. What matters is that you attain your goal. The Way of the warrior is to slay the enemy by cutting him down without delay. You must have utter resolve in order to do this and you must constantly sharpen your skills. Eventually you will understand the way to do things effectively and efficiently without stress or strain. Mislead the enemy, and then slay him with an unorthodox technique.

## TO MOVE AS A SHADOW

Sometimes you cannot go straight in to the enemy and it is necessary to feint just prior to attacking strongly. If the enemy is very strong, he may not show his spirit. Because of this, it is essential that you make a "misdirecting" motion to open up the enemy, forcing him to show you his strengths and weaknesses. You must constantly be aware of your surroundings and be able to capitalize upon them. If you make an opening, then you absolutely must go for it or it is a waste of the "spirit of the thing." If you practice otherwise, after a while you will be unable to take advantage of an enemy's weaknesses and become ineffective as a warrior. You will certainly lose the Way. Study this carefully.

## TO SUFFOCATE A SHADOW

What is meant by suffocating a shadow is to understand the enemy's strengths and easily see through his intentions. If you can see what the enemy is planning, then how can you fail to defeat him instantly? Only by failing to take advantage of the situation can you, in turn, be defeated. You must train constantly to understand the reasoning behind this strategy. There is nothing mystical in this strategy. If you show the enemy that you know what he is planning, he can be forced to change his attitude to one that is favorable to you. When you see his change in attitude, immediately thrust in with a killing strike. Beat his timing with your timing. Beat his approach with your approach. Control the situation at all times by being aware of your surroundings. When you study the Way, it will come to you that everything I am speaking of is practical and functional. Problems occur when you do not understand the true Way of the warrior and fail to act upon opportunity.

## TO IMPRESS YOUR ATTITUDE

Attitudes are contagious. To impress your attitude on the enemy is to force him to think in terms that are to your advantage. When you understand your own abilities, you are able to pass them along to others in the same way a teacher can pass along correct and incorrect ideas and teachings. If you show the enemy that you are agitated then he may become calmer and, at that instant, attack with the utter resolve and conviction that will kill you. You must have success in your heart and mind in order to know whether information is true or false. If you cannot do this, then you must take the time to study further if you are so inclined. Do not be impressed by the enemy's attitude. Remain calm even if he starts to attack. If you do not follow yourself, then you will certainly follow someone else. The whole idea of warfare is to beat the enemy. The strength and courage of your convictions is what will carry you through every time, regardless of the situation. You must understand this. Without hard study, how can you ever hope to acknowledge yourself as your own supreme master? This comes with long practice, study, and devotion to the art. The "spirit of the thing itself" will reveal this to you. When you have imparted your attitudes to someone else, that person effectively becomes your follower. This is the Way of the warrior. When you do not discern the reality of the truth, then you become foolish. Do not rush yourself in your learning and do not expect to know what the master understands. In the case of an enemy, it is important that you control that person or you can be beaten in battle.

---

## FORCING LOSS OF BALANCE

A warrior can lose his balance because of danger, surprise, or difficulty. When you attack, you should do so with no warning of any kind. Once your enemy loses his balance, your attack will be virtually impossible to stop. If you stand strong and rigid, your spirit will be very easy to read and you will be beaten because you are not flexible. The same is true of being too loose. Flexibility is a very important attitude. Things will not always go your way regardless of your practice and your attempts to define your own existence. Therefore, how can you always maintain strictly one posture? In large scale combat, attack where the enemy is not expecting you to. Likewise, in one-to-one combat appear to be one thing and then attack as another. Never give the enemy a chance to see your true spirit. It is easy to lead a horse when you know how to hold the reins. When your enemies are deceived, you will be able to control any situation because they are expecting one thing and you strike at them with another. It is the same with feigning a punch and throwing a kick.

## SCARING THE ENEMY

The difference between a half-hearted scream intended to scare the enemy off and a resolute shout is the difference between bragging and making a commitment to attack with the intent to kill. If you constantly scream, then you will be perceived as a screamer and not a doer. However, if you maintain a strong and powerful presence and then commit yourself to the attack with a forceful shout, you will scare the enemy and win easily. You win with resolute power and not with false appearances. When you have scared the enemy and his rhythm is confused, you can easily go in for the kill. Use your voice, your body, and your sword to scare him. To frighten the enemy means to make him lose his balance, providing you with an opening into his defenses where he is easily slain if you have the mind to kill him.

## TO FLOOD IN

If the fight develops to the point where neither you nor the enemy are able to make the killing strike, you will have the advantage if you suddenly change your technical strategy and proceed relentlessly with your attack. This is called "flooding in." To back off and try to regain your composure gives the enemy the opportunity to do likewise; it then starts all over again. When you are in a fight, you are not in a contest to see who can outlast the other in a standoff.

This is why you absolutely must train incessantly to develop the proper spirit that will enable you to continue attacking even under dire circumstances. It is not a question of your technical ability, but it certainly is a matter of your desire to win with the spirit of the warrior—something you can attain only when you have acknowledged the Way as the true reality for you and you alone.

## TO CHIP AWAY THE EDGES

Sometimes you must make sacrifices in your attack in order to weaken the enemy and chip away at his defenses. If you find that it is difficult for you to penetrate strong armor, then go to the areas where the armor is weak and you will eventually break through. There are weak spots in all armor. If you continue to chip away at the weak spots in the enemy's armor, he will eventually weaken and lose balance. The reason there are weak spots in armor is because these are the places that have to be "open" in order to provide flexibility in the enemy's movements. Go to these areas and slowly whittle him down; when you have the opportunity to go in for the kill, strike with absolute conviction. Do not hesitate. Destroy the enemy!

## CONFUSING THE ENEMY

Confusing the enemy is achieved by forcing him to constantly redirect his efforts. With proper feints and thrusts, you can get the enemy thinking about where the attack will be coming from. Causing confusion in the enemy means making him unable to concentrate on his attack, permitting you to come in with a well executed killing strike. I have spoken before about feinting and striking, misdirecting the enemy's thoughts, forcing him to think the wrong thing, and I will continue to repeat it over and over again. It is essential that you control the enemy and make slaying him a simple thing to do. You should be starting to understand what being a warrior is all about by this time. You must be fully resolved to kill the enemy by any means. You must practice constantly to understand these principles until they become second nature. The warrior attitude is very simple. Focus your mind on your goal, constantly strive to attain perfection, and do not allow yourself to be sidetracked. Think only of winning. You must maintain your own ideals and study properly or you will be sure to lose the Way.

## THREE FIERCE SHOUTS

There are only three times when you can scream fiercely in combat: before, during and after. Shouting and screaming are the same as long as they fulfill their purpose, which is to terrify the enemy. At the beginning of a battle, you should shout to unsettle the enemy. During the battle, you should shout during each attack to maintain your own resoluteness of spirit. After you have slain the enemy, you should shout to indicate your winning resolve to honor the "spirit of the thing itself." You should practice with a strong inner to outer shout at all times, as loud and as forcefully as you can. Never shout before or after a particular technique is executed, but rather at the moment you are making the strike. This helps to maintain rhythm. The shout and the strike are not two different things. They are both parts of the same thing. Think this through. It is most important to understand. When breathing, concentrate on pulling air into the lower abdominal area to develop a powerful source of energy, and never hold back on your shout for any reason. This will build up internal stress that can steal power away from you. On the other hand, do not always go around shouting because this will make you seem to have no control over what you are trying to accomplish with your shout. Always shout when you go into an attack. Always shout when you are defending an attack prior to reversing the situation. And always shout in victory after you have finished killing the enemy; in this way, you will be able to quickly relax from the tension of battle.

---

## TO MOVE WITH THE ENEMY

**W**hen you go into the attack you are essentially telling the enemy that you don't think very highly of his spirit. This is a very powerful attitude and must be developed carefully from much practice and technical ability. When you have this attitude, it is obvious to the enemy and he will react with hesitation and confusion. In large group fighting, you must constantly maintain the attitude of attack without showing any indication of retreat, regardless of the situation you are in. No matter what the enemy attempts to do, do not give him a moment's rest. Do not forget that actual combat is extremely fast and demands that you act and react without thinking. Moving with the enemy means not permitting him to regather his thoughts when in retreat. When you permit the enemy to regather himself, you are releasing your control of the situation and allowing the enemy a chance to defeat you.

---

## TO CRUSH THE ENEMY'S BODY AND SPIRIT

**C**rushing the enemy's body and spirit means you degrade and humiliate him the instant before going in for the kill. Your concentration upon destroying the enemy must be intense and single-minded. What is the sense in fighting if you do not go in for the kill immediately? Any hesitation is foolish and lends itself to boasting. This can get you killed. When you see weakness in the enemy's armor, go at it and do not stop the attack until the enemy is dead. Otherwise he may recover and be able to regather his thoughts and spirit and turn the tide of battle against you. When you go for the kill—kill. Without mercy. Your spirit must be enormous. Think this through carefully.

## THE MOON AND STARS

What is meant by the moon and stars is that although both are in the sky they are two different things. The sky is the attack and the moon and stars are the methods to be used. There should be no thought about using only one method or the other. You attack with a technique and it does not work. You try it again and it still does not work. Switch! You must never rely on only one particular attitude to get a job done. The enemy may be prepared for this technique in a way that you may not have anticipated, so it is indeed foolish to try to continue with it. When you change your technique in the midst of battle, you are essentially becoming better able to kill because your spirit is not being forced into any one position.

## REACHING INTO THE ABYSS

Reaching into the abyss means that you must always beat the enemy in both body and spirit. When you have merely beaten the enemy superficially, he may still be able to regain composure and regather his thoughts, thereby strengthening his spirit to beat you. At times it may be difficult for you to continue with your attack when the enemy is not yet beaten in body and spirit, but it is precisely at this time that you must reach into the abyss and bring yourself to the point where you are able to totally destroy the enemy. By reaching into the abyss of yourself, you are able to reach into the abyss of the enemy and slay him properly and with the correct execution of purpose. If you permit the enemy to regain composure, then he certainly will attack again. To reach into the abyss of the enemy is to halt any additional attempts on the enemy's part to continue the fight. All attacks must therefore be executed with great resolve. This is accomplished only through practice and meditation on the Way of the warrior.

## TO START AGAIN

In practice one should consider the possibility of being unable to beat the enemy with whatever means you have been using. This can and does happen. Starting again means to come to an impasse in your efforts to kill the enemy but then immediately abandoning your approach by taking another strategy, refreshing your spirit, and starting again. When you have to change your spirit while in combat, you must do so without stopping the flow of battle. In order to enable yourself to change your approach, you must constantly practice all sorts of variations on the same attack. In this way, you will be able to change in the middle of a fight.

### SNAKE'S HEAD, SNAKE'S TAIL

Sometimes both spirits in a fight can become entangled and nothing seems to work. Think of strategy as being both a snake's head and a snake's tail. Never permit yourself to become entangled in the small points of combat. Expand your spirit and see both the large and the small. Do not become stricken with a single-minded attitude. This is fatal. You must be able to function flexibly within the structure of the one thing you are doing. You must understand that there is more than one path to the top of the mountain. However, you must also realize the importance of staying within the bounds of the Way you are traversing. Only then can you truly understand the need to be aware of other attitudes.

## COMMANDERS KNOW THE ENEMY TROOPS

**W**ho is it that controls the battle? Is it you or is it the enemy? That the commander must know the enemy troops is a vital aspect of my strategy. Whether in one-man battles or large-group battles, you must understand the enemy. If the commander knows the spirit of the enemy, he can easily control them and quickly beat them. To win with ease, you must maintain control over the enemy's actions. Not doing so permits the enemy to control you. If neither of you have an understanding of the Way, the fight is meaningless and the outcome will be governed by luck, the winner also being the loser, regardless of the physical outcome because of the cost of the battle. You must control the fight by possessing a greater spirit than that of your enemy. Understand this strategy and master it.

## RELEASING BOTH HOLDS

**W**hat is meant by releasing both holds is that the warrior does not depend on anything but himself to beat the enemy. Do not rely on any particular weapon. Posture and attitude can often win battles. Embody the spirit of winning by having the spirit to win. It is not always necessary to go into physical combat to win a fight. Sometimes you can win by your presence alone. Other times you can win simply by letting the enemy know your intentions. Think this through very carefully. It is the essence of strategy.

## THE BODY AND SPIRIT OF STONE

**W**hen you truly understand the Way, you can take any form that you want to. It is almost as if you had developed miraculous powers. You can become as light as a feather, as fluid as water, or as stiff as a board. Regardless of the form you take, once you have understood my strategy you can not be beaten by one man or ten thousand. Your "attitude/no-attitude" cannot be stirred except from within. Once you have understood my strategy you will be a warrior to be reckoned with.

## THOUGHTS ABOUT MY BOOK OF FIRE

**T**his book can be considered a path to spiritual understanding for the warrior who truly wishes to understand the Way of the warrior. My heart and soul have been devoted to the Way of strategy ever since I was a young man. I have constantly studied ways to train my hands and eyes. Through constant practice, I have come to understand the spiritual aspects of my strategy.

When I watch men from other schools and listen to them talking about their theories, I can tell they haven't the slightest idea of what my strategy is about. They prefer to act out their techniques and think they accomplish things without proper practice. These men are fools. They try to impress their non-understanding upon the uninitiated. More and more men are practicing this way and that is why the true Way is becoming meaningless and will eventually be lost to all men except through my teachings.

The only thing of importance in the Way of strategy is the willingness and ability to truly defeat the enemy in actual combat with a long sword. If you understand what I am telling you in these pages, you will never lose to anyone. You will always win.

So ends the Book of Fire.

# THE BOOK OF
# WIND

trategy demands that you know the difference between yourself and others. The Book of Wind discusses the prevalent attitudes among other schools. In order for one school to be compared to another, both must exist. Each school has its good points and its bad points. Some schools use the attitudes of strength, some schools lean towards only one or two types of techniques, and some schools rely on a constant expansion of the number of techniques a warrior uses. The main idea of my school is that it is based on the development of the Way through an expression of the spirit, techniques notwithstanding.

I want to clearly explain the good and bad points of other schools. My school is different. I care not for the dressings of other uniforms or the growing of small trees, although these things have their place. If the school is primarily interested in building up a clientele and displays the trophies won at tournaments (among other things) it gives the student the wrong idea about the Way of the warrior. Essentially, such a school is trying to sell its wares to the public by using the long sword as a means to accumulate wealth. This is absolutely *not* the Way of the warrior. You must understand this if you are to develop your spirit in the proper manner. The "spirit of the thing itself" revolts against this type of thinking and reveals "itself" falsely to the practitioner who believes that showing off is the essence of strategy. To be a warrior is one of the most painstaking callings you can choose in this life. Combat is not a game. It is life and death. It simply cannot be otherwise.

It is not enough merely to insist upon proper carriage of the body and false brandishing of weapons and the spirit. For while it is obvious that carriage and technique are important, they are not important enough to win fights of a mortal nature. The spirit must be cultivated; if it is not, a tragic shortcoming of awareness in the warrior will result.

It is important to understand the reasons and philosophies of other systems in order to truly benefit from my own. I do not hesitate to point these things out to you. Without comparison you have no reference point with which to judge for yourself and decide how to properly develop your own self. You should study the ways of others to reinforce your own understanding of yourself. Constantly reevaluate yourself.

## SCHOOLS THAT USE AN EXTRA LONG SWORD

Other schools, because they teach a method that relies on distance between themselves and the enemy, are generally unable to close in on the enemy easily. They are afraid of going in to the enemy and defeating him with one stroke. They think the length of their weapon can offer them additional security in combat. Yet the extra length only hinders their resolve. This alone makes them weak. They are weak, and if they fought someone from my Ichi school, they would very simply be closed in on and defeated.

Fighting from a distance without the advantage of strategy prevents the warrior from becoming one with his true self. Fighting this way separates the body and the spirit and is therefore not effective in fights to the death. Certainly it is advantageous to have the edge in distance or speed, but without proper understanding of strategy these so-called advantages become weapons that can be used against you. If you truly understand strategy, then you simply do not need advantages as such. You cannot rely on your weapons alone, though you must be able to wield them thoroughly, applying their nature with the correct execution and form. Your resolve must be intense and your courage steadfast. You must go in to the attack in order to win the fight. This is the Way.

A short sword can easily beat an extra long sword. Essentially, the weapon in and of itself is meaningless without the proper application of its virtues by the warrior. Keep in mind there are martial arts that have been developed to provide unarmed self-defense against a warrior wearing armor and wielding a sword. An unarmed warrior can beat an armed warrior if my strategy is understood. So again, it is the development of the spirit that carries you through battle and makes you victorious.

When a warrior uses an extra long sword, it is difficult for him to come in close and dispatch the enemy swiftly. If a man is unable to function because of his choice of weapon, then he is easily defeated. This does not mean that you should disregard the virtue of an extra long sword. Everything has its value, even if it is not apparent to you.

You must always be prepared to deal with every situation, regardless of how you are equipped. This means with the long sword, the short sword, no sword, or an extra long sword. My personal preference is for the long sword. It is important to understand the differences in weapons and the places they can be used.

Even so, it is not altogether impossible for someone with an extra long sword to be able to do exquisite battle in an inappropriate place. Consider this possibility. Being aware of the conditions of others does not automatically make you superior. Circumstances being equal, the winner of the fight is still the one with the most resoluteness. It is essential for a student on the path of the warrior never to close his mind to the possibilities of other possibilities.

## THE STRONG SWORD SPIRIT AND THE WEAK SWORD SPIRIT IN OTHER SCHOOLS

This passage is one of the most important parts of the entire Five Rings. It is also one of the most difficult concepts of strategy to understand and to come to realize. Your strength is not your own, nor is your speed. Forcing yourself to cut more strongly than is necessary will result in a possible loss of control of your weapon. Attempting to strike overly fast can also cause you to lose your balance. Strategy is based on quickness and not speed, power not strength. In practice you must remember to attack naturally. In developing technique you must practice naturally. It is constant practice that will make you unbeatable in combat, whether it is with one man or on a large scale. The true "spirit of the thing itself" always knows exactly what it has to do to protect the vehicle that it is expressing "itself" through. Who cares how strong you are anyway? Someone you are trying to impress? If you continue on in this thinking you will lose the meaning of the Way of the warrior, which is never easy to attain in the best of cases. So why would you want to jeopardize yourself by showing off? You only have to make sure that you kill the enemy before the enemy kills you. That is your function. It is the function of "the thing itself" to perform the technique in accordance with what is really necessary to destroy the enemy. This very simple truth is one of the hardest aspects of learning the Way of the warrior. Total non-commitment to yourself—only commitment to the Way.

In combat you are not in a contest of strength and you are not in a race. You are there for the only purpose there is to be in combat—to kill the enemy. Showing extra strength indicates weakness in your technique. It also shows a lack of control on your part because you are depending on something outside of your true self. Your own preconceived ideas of what being "strong" means is not the Way of the warrior. That is why you see the "older" masters able to defeat everyone in the school with what appears to be no effort. The important thing to remember here is not to rely on anything other than your true spirit and the skill that you have developed through constant practice without the benefit of impressing anyone while you were practicing.

The Way insists that you learn to use the enemy's strength

as your own. The only reason a warrior is alive is to fight, and the only reason a warrior fights is to win. Otherwise, why be a warrior? It is easier to count beads.

---

## THE IMPORTANCE OF THE LONG SWORD OVER THE SHORT SWORD

Superior warriors have no preference for using a long sword or a short sword. A sword is used to strike down an enemy. Warriors can use any weapon they choose if they understand my strategy. It is also to be understood that using only a short sword means that you are waiting for an unguarded moment in your enemy before attacking. This is not good because it is merely a defensive posture and does not fully realize the true meaning of strategy. You are waiting for the opportunity to be offered to take the initiative. Using a short sword means you are going into the enemy's defenses too closely and you may not be able to handle multiple attackers. The short sword will also cause you to become entangled with the enemy. To constantly be on the defensive means that you are weak in your resolve and that you do not truly understand the Way of the warrior. The attitude at all times is to go in to the attack. To do this you must be properly prepared both mentally and physically. This includes understanding your weaponry. To continuously fend off an attacker without the resolution to kill him is a great waste of time, effort, and energy. You must remember this. You are not there to play and you are not there to show off. You are there to kill the enemy or as many enemies as is necessary. If you constantly practice with the spirit of killing the enemy, you will never have to be concerned with the methods of other schools.

It is best to understand the proper use of the long sword. To win in fights you must control the enemy and not necessarily rely on your weapons so much as on your intelligence. You must chase the enemy around and strive to confuse him by making him lose his balance. You must stand straight and true with your spine erect. You must understand what it means to suffocate him with a pillow. Then kill him. There is nothing else. Most people trying to learn strategy do not understand this for some reason. They think that countering or evading or running is the Way of strategy. It is not.

Early on in training your teacher must impart this wisdom to you. If he does not, perhaps he is the wrong teacher for you if you truly wish to learn the Way of strategy. The true warrior is unflinching in his devotion to studying his craft.

If you are unfortunate enough to have never had this vital concept drummed into your head, consider yourself lucky for having it done now. It is a terrible thing that many other schools do not understand what the Way of the warrior really is. Many warriors have had to take a hard look at reality when it became evident to them that they were not being "led to the path" but perhaps only being "led down the path."

## SCHOOLS THAT TEACH ODD METHODS
## OF USING THE LONG SWORD

*C*lever people do not understand temperance of spirit. Clever techniques shown to beginning students in other schools are very dangerous to the unformed mind. They seek to trick people by dancing and jumping and switching hands. This is stupidity and it does nothing to enhance the reputation of the warrior. It is because of these people that commoners despise the warrior mentality, for commoners are not shown the true Way. Clever people teach that no one can beat them because of their superior technique. They belittle others who have different methods. They try to bully others into following their Way. Some teachers think that by impressing students with their own skills they can convert them to their way of thinking. These are terrible things to do and I despise those who practice this method of teaching. They do not understand the true Way of the warrior. They have probably not had experience in real battle and only play at what they do. In the heat of battle the "spirit of the thing itself" will reveal its disgust towards those who practice in this manner. They will lose the Way and be beaten in fights.

There is only one way to kill the enemy. The Way is to kill the enemy with one stroke. Killing by "cutting" is totally different from killing by "slashing," "slashing" being every other way to kill besides that of the warrior "cut." Anyone can kill anyone for any reason at any time. It is foolish to think that someone who is untrained cannot kill. The Way of the warrior is to kill as a Way of being and not merely for the result itself. Strategy teaches the appropriate manner in which to kill correctly and without hesitation. The intense training that a warrior goes through teaches this simple lesson. Being known as a warrior is a very substantive thing. It is never taken lightly, especially by other warriors, if they are true warriors and not merely braggarts from another school or system.

To practice your craft as a warrior takes a tremendous amount of devotion and you must understand the need for frustration while you are training. Few can understand this, to their discredit.

You absolutely must believe in what you are doing and you must practice it with the intention of laying down your life for it, if the "spirit of the thing itself" requires you to do so. The reason true warriors are fierce is because their training is fierce. Ponder this over and over.

Regardless, you must maintain the proper form and balance while training and while not training. Maintain respect for others and respect for your own way. Not to do so is moronic. Maintain the proper attitudes towards the Way and permit the Way to proceed through you based on your own resolve. The method is to go straight in and it is undoubtedly the hardest method to master. That is why you must constantly practice and not merely take up the sword as a novel way of spending time. You can, of course, if you only want to make a hobby out of attaining perfection. That, however, is not the true Way.

## INCORRECT CARRIAGE AND
## WARRIOR ATTITUDES

D o not bear false attitudes. False attitudes work best where there are no enemies. In real situations they can get you killed very quickly. The true warrior does not go around telling everyone he is a great warrior. He permits his actions to govern others' responses. My idea of attitude is based on the principle of the true Way, which is to not allow it to be perceived by the enemy. Blatant attitudes such as fancy armor, engraved weapons in battle array and the like are an attempt to throw an enemy off balance. Yet these things only impress the untrained and irresolute. The warrior's attitude is that of taking the lead in a fight and winning with resolve. You must understand this basic lesson.

It is important to perceive the enemy's attitudes, regardless of whether you deem him to be correct or incorrect in having them. You should not judge the enemy's attitudes needlessly. What you should do is use them to your advantage by throwing him into confusion and making him lose balance. This can be your way of scaring him and forcing him to act according to your needs. It is stupid to try to beat his attitude with your attitude. This is another form of bragging and results in hesitation on your part in going in for the kill, the reason you are there in the first place. The warrior always wants to control the situation in a battle. This is why it is necessary to practice diligently to attain the consciousness required to maintain this "attitude."

It is required of a warrior that in order to follow the true

Way he be aware of all possible conditions prior to the actual battle taking place; in this way he may not even have to do battle because of his superior intelligence based on perception and intuition. It is possible to win a fight without ever having to go into combat. You must understand this.

Bearing an attack well, even when you are superior in physical strength, is not the proper attitude for the warrior to follow. Try to understand this. If you wait for the attack, defend against it, and only then go in for the attack by parrying and striking, you are making extra work for yourself. Moreover, there is always the possibility of missing the "block." If you approach the enemy with the attitude of defeating him without delay and with utter resolve, then you will certainly be in a better position to finish him off with quicker timing. When you go into an attack and are committed to destroying the enemy, you do not have to "worry" about being cut in return; and therefore you won't be. The "spirit of the thing itself" is what carries you through to a successful resolution of a fight. When you are returning the attack to the enemy after he has attacked you, you are permitting your rhythm and timing to be controlled by him. Regardless of how well you fight, you are on the defensive. You should strive to be neither offensive nor defensive. These ideas can force the mind to stop in its flow of consciousness and get you killed when you are in a fight. I strongly urge you to understand this part of my strategy if you are on the path of the warrior.

## FIXING THE EYES IN OTHER SCHOOLS

Some teachers say that you should always stare at the enemy's weapons, or at his eyes, or at his feet. This is not a good idea because it fixes your spirit in place and is easily read by an experienced fighter. It also limits your ability to be flexible under any circumstances. It takes the naturalness out of your actions and weakens your resolve. If the football player constantly watches only the football, how can he ever expect to run with it down the field and score? If the master musician looks only at the music, note for note, how can he ever play with the "soul" required for the music to make sense? It is the same with the warrior; one particular part of the enemy should not be stared at. This makes it too easy for the enemy to deceive you and interfere with your timing and rhythm. You should favor the broader view.

Your eyes should be fixed on no-thing. Your stare should be unfixed. When I fight another man, I look through him and think only of making the hit. I have no preconceived notions of which target is the one to aim for. I let nature take its course and permit the "spirit of the thing itself" to express "itself" through me and make me the victor. And I never forget to acknowledge the "spirit" after I have won a fight. This is the true warrior's Way.

With experience you will soon learn to ascertain the strength and speed of the enemy. This will enable you to figure out his intentions and determine his skill. Look through the enemy, look through his heart, look beyond his very being and degrade him entirely with your spirit. That is what you must concentrate upon. The "spirit of the thing itself" will guide your hands accordingly and help you to beat the enemy in a fight.

Always take the broader view of the entire situation both when you are in a fight and when you are not. Do not concentrate on details. Keep only one thing in mind: that thing is to beat the enemy. In this way your spirit will continue to grow and you will always be conscious of your surroundings and the situations that appear. Concentrating on one cart when you are crossing the avenue means that you leave yourself open to another cart hitting you from the other side because you were concentrating on details and not the entire situation. The same applies to fighting. If you constantly gaze at the enemy's feet, it will be easy for him to strike you with a punch. If you concentrate on the hands, he will kick you. If you concentrate on the eyes, he can easily fool you into thinking one thing while he does another. Always look to the mountain and beyond. This way you will be aware of the broader picture and can easily win if you have the resolve to do so.

## THE STUPIDITY OF FANCY FOOTWORK

D o not attempt to be clever with your feet. Many attitudes of footwork seem to me to be simple wastes of time because their only intention is to get your attention and throw you into confusion. Likewise, when you shuffle your feet or make quick little jumps to the side (or make any useless moves), you lose your advantage against a skilled fighter. Besides, you are not there to dance. You are there to kill the enemy. Again, the emphasis is on not relying on a specific "walking" or "moving" pattern. The definitions of the types of walks reflect their users and are to be considered as indicating the spirit in which they are used. For example, a jumping pattern indicates a jumpy spirit, don't you think?

When I move in on the enemy, I move with resolve and surefootedness. I walk in as naturally as if I were walking in the street. I do not differentiate between walking in to attack or walking into the house.

My strategy does not permit change in composure, regardless of the ground being fought on. By being surefooted I can overcome most obstacles in my path. This way I do not lose my rhythm. When I make changes in rhythm it is based on the enemy's rhythm, and by moving fast or slow I close in on him and kill him.

Why would you want to change your basic attitudes towards life simply because a new set of events is occurring? If you take the time to change your methodology in midstream your spirit has to catch up, regardless of how quickly you move. Eventually you are going to have to come back to your natural state. So why leave it in the first place?

You must maintain a natural rhythm and a natural timing. Anything that you add to or delete from this naturalness will cost you the advantage when you are proceeding to destroy the enemy. Moving in a natural gait will afford you the opportunity to move either fast or slow and will thus enable you to follow the enemy with a much steadier attitude. Your spirit will remain intact and you will be able to defeat the enemy.

## HOW TO THINK OF SPEED

Some schools think that speed it all that is necessary to win fights. If you can make a fast slash and win, all the better. I do not agree with this idea and think that it in fact slows you down. You are again relying on an external concept. What is speed anyway? Speed is relative to the situation in which you are involved. Being fast or being slow has to do with speed. Quickness is what you want in your spirit. A quick spirit is able to overcome any apparent speed with which an enemy is coming at you. Quickness gets inside of speed and enables you to control the situation by killing the enemy. When you advance, you advance quickly and get immediately to the point. Your speed is dependent upon the speed of the enemy. You adjust yourself accordingly and do not think in terms of being faster or slower. Quickness is the thing that counts. What is more, if you are constantly moving fast you will have no time to maintain your poise and timing. Your rhythm will start to get out of control because you will tire and start to move slower, perhaps without even realizing it.

When you are skilled in the art you have chosen to study, you will have the true understanding of rhythm and timing necessary to perform flawlessly. Perfection can only be based on true calmness within the soul and any attempt to radically change for no good reason will throw the entire attitude of calmness out of harmony. Move naturally and gracefully. Execute correctly. Think about this.

Quickness is the thing on which the spirit relies. Speed, not being necessarily good, can only cause you to lose your control. If you move too fast or too slowly, you may give your enemy the advantage necessary to beat you. Always move naturally and calmly, with great resolve to destroy the enemy.

In a large battle with many men, everyone will move with their own rhythm and timing. Not being influenced by others is essential if you are to be able to beat men in a fight. You absolutely must train diligently in this regard. When you are your own self and are not concerned with the motions of others, you will be in control of the situation and in control of the enemy and the movements with which he may or may not attack you. Keeping calm is essential to not losing sight of your main purpose in a fight, to kill the enemy quickly.

## INNER AND OUTER ATTITUDES
## IN OTHER SCHOOLS

The difference between a warrior's victory in combat and an exemplary artistic performance is that in art the outcome does not include the death of a dancer in the dance or the death of the musician in the performance, while, in combat, the reality is that the outcome is decided with the death of the enemy or yourself.

I do not like inner and outer attitudes. They are detrimental to understanding the true nature of the universe, which is oneness. Why confuse yourself with definitions of what you think the "spirit of the thing itself" should be doing?

When I teach beginners, I concentrate on developing technique and make little mention of deeper principles. They are not necessary and intellectual exercises tend to limit the student's progress. Only later, when they are able to understand that fighting is not an intellectual exercise (although the aesthetics involved in executing specific techniques call for a strong and intelligent spirit), will I go into the deeper meaning of things.

If you concern yourself with an "inner" and an "outer" attitude, you will only interfere with your timing and your rhythm. It is best to concentrate only on killing the enemy and attaining perfection in yourself and your technique.

## ENDNOTES TO THE BOOK OF THE WIND

It is not wise to criticize another's Way. There are reasons for each man to have his own. Ask someone a question and he will give you an answer. Ask the same question to another and he will give a different answer. There is no need to examine the doctrines of another school of thought until you have come to terms with the doctrines of the school you are studying. In the very beginning you seek a teacher. Then you come to understand the realities of what it is you are studying. When you feel that something is missing or that you

are not learning anything further, you must of your own voli-
tion seek the next level of instruction. There is no such thing
as Yin-Yang. This is not to say that Yin-Yang does not exist.

So ends the Book of Wind.

# THE BOOK OF
# NO-THING

My Way of strategy is recorded in the Book of No-Thing. The spirit of the universe is an emptiness which is no-thing. Man can have no understanding of this place. It exists and is, but yet it is not. If you know something, you know something. If you do not know something, it does not exist in your world. In the universe, no-thing-ness is not a thing that is true and not a thing that is not true.

When men of the world look at things with the wrong perception and do not understand what they see, they say it is the place of no-thing-ness. This is incorrect thinking. The idea that men who study strategy and do not understand no-thing-ness do not, therefore, understand their craft is not correct either. Everything is revealed to all men as they desire it to be revealed to them, by their own definitions alone.

If you hope to understand my strategy you must study as many of the martial arts as you can and never veer from your chosen course. Your everyday practice, as it accumulates, will eventually reveal true no-thing-ness to you as the "spirit of the thing itself." When you have truly understood the universe in relation to your art and your art in relation to the universe, you will come to understand no-thing-ness. This may appear to be a very difficult concept to understand, but it is quite simple. Do not take anything for granted and do not put emphasis on the things of men. In this way understand my strategy.

No matter how hard you study, if you do not become one with the art you pursue you can never truly be one with the universe and the "spirit of the thing itself" will always elude you. Things will never appear to be what they truly are. But if you look at things with no attachment to them you will come to understand your place. The work is more important than the worker. When you come to see things in a broader perspective, taking no-thing-ness to be the truth, you will see truth as no-thing.

There is virtue in the universe but it should not be confused with good and evil. Wisdom exists, principles exist, and the Way of the warrior exists, but spirit is no-thing-ness.

Based upon my own understanding of the Way of the warrior and my own understanding of the universe, I am presenting the entire matter of the Book of No-thing as one idea.

Let me repeat it again. The Way of the warrior is based on no-thing-ness. No-thing-ness is not to be understood as a "thing" because it then would be based on a conception of something, which would not be no-thing. The Zen term for "no-thing" which is the closest we can come to defining "no-thing" is called *Mu*. To understand *Mu* is to understand no-thing. It is essential to be careful with intellectual definitions at this point. The issue is clear and I explain it as well as anyone else. Even without the literal translation of my *Book of*

*Five Rings*, you can come close to understanding no-thing by realizing that there is nothing outside of yourself that can ever enable you to get better, stronger, richer, quicker, or smarter. Everything is within. Everything exists. Seek nothing outside of yourself.

If you understand what exists then you can understand that which does not exist. This means that although it is impossible to know that which does not exist, it is possible to know that if "anything is anything, then everything is everything." In the Way of the warrior there is no such thing as thought (other than the intellectual powers you need to come to understand this terminology). The spirit is no-thing-ness means that there is no such thing as relying upon anything at all outside of your individual mind.

Zen masters use little stories to bewilder their students. These are called *koans*. They are specifically inane in their presentation, but when students come to understand no-thing-ness they will also come to understand the *koans*.

I could go on and on forever in trying to explain no-thing-ness, but that would be exactly the wrong way to approach it.

The Zen point of view suggests that you stop all conceptual thinking. Stop thinking about what you "feel" is right or wrong. Quite frankly, because all the universe is simply no-thing-ness (or *Mu*), there is no reason to pursue any attempt at perfection. Perfection is all there is and when you come to realize this, you will have understood my Way of strategy and the Way of the warrior, at which time you can forget about it and just be "it." Best to have it put this way. Simply be!

*YOU* are the Spirit of the Thing Itself!

Thus ends the Book of No-thing and the *Book of Five Rings.*

# ABOUT THE AUTHOR

## Stephen F. Kaufman, Hanshi, 10th Dan

An acknowledged Founding Father of American Karate, Hanshi Kaufman originally trained on Okinawa in the 1950s and has held the title of Hanshi since 1991. He is the founder of Hebi-ryu karate do: Dojo no Hebi, School of the Snake. He has taught for military organizations, law enforcement agencies, and many community centers and public agencies. Hanshi lectures and teaches strategy and motivation throughout the world.

He is the author of many books, including *Musashi's Book of Five Rings*, *Sun Tzu's Art of War*, *The Shogun Scrolls*, *The Living Tao* and *Zen and the Art of Stickfighting*. His latest works, *Sword in the Boardroom* and *Formal Hebi-ryu Combat Karate Studies*, are soon to be released. Hanshi's books have been translated into many languages.

Hanshi can be contacted at PO Box 135, Lenox Sta., NYC, NY 10021 or email: hanshi@hanshi.com. His websites are www.hanshi.com and www.hanshi.com/seminar.